DARK PSYCHOLOGY

Preventive Techniques for Managing Being Manipulated

(Learn How to Decode People Personalities by Knowing Body Language)

Douglas Hecht

Published by Sharon Lohan

© **Douglas Hecht**

All Rights Reserved

Dark Psychology: Preventive Techniques for Managing Being Manipulated (Learn How to Decode People Personalities by Knowing Body Language)

ISBN 978-1-990334-57-3

All rights reserved. No part of this guide may be reproduced in any form without permission in writing from the publisher except in the case of brief quotations embodied in critical articles or reviews.

Legal & Disclaimer

The information contained in this book is not designed to replace or take the place of any form of medicine or professional medical advice. The information in this book has been provided for educational and entertainment purposes only.

The information contained in this book has been compiled from sources deemed reliable, and it is accurate to the best of the Author's knowledge; however, the Author cannot guarantee its accuracy and validity and cannot be held liable for any errors or omissions. Changes are periodically made to this book. You must consult your doctor or get professional medical advice before using any of the suggested remedies, techniques, or information in this book.

Upon using the information contained in this book, you agree to hold harmless the Author from and against any damages, costs, and expenses, including any legal fees potentially resulting from the application of any of the information provided by this guide. This disclaimer applies to any damages or injury caused by the use and application, whether directly or indirectly, of any advice or information presented, whether for breach of contract, tort, negligence, personal injury, criminal intent, or under any other cause of action.

You agree to accept all risks of using the information presented inside this book. You need to consult a professional medical practitioner in order to ensure you are both able and healthy enough to participate in this program.

Table of Contents

INTRODUCTION 1

CHAPTER 1: WHAT IS DARK PSYCHOLOGY? 2

CHAPTER 2: MANIPULATION 27

CHAPTER 3: THE MAKE-UP OF A MANIPULATOR 61

CHAPTER 4: EFFECTS OF DARK PSYCHOLOGY 80

CHAPTER 5: STOP THE MANIPULATORS 87

CHAPTER 6: HISTORY OF PERSUASION 100

CHAPTER 7: HOW TO SPOT A FELLOW MANIPULATOR .. 109

CHAPTER 8: MIND CONTROL 129

CHAPTER 9: THE TROJAN IN YOUR HEAD 141

CHAPTER 10: DEVELOPING MIND CONTROL 158

CHAPTER 11: SOME OTHER CONSPIRACY THEORIES (SOME ABSURD, SOME CREDIBLE) 187

CONCLUSION 204

Introduction

The topic of psychology is one that draws the attention of millions of human beings all over the world and has become quintessential in matters of both health and justice. Sadly, psychology also has a negative impression around it that makes people hesitate before trusting their psychological mind and concerns with the expertise of others. In most cases, this hesitation comes from a lack of familiarity or understanding of what psychology is and how it can be used to improve people's everyday lives.

Chapter 1: What Is Dark Psychology?

According to psychologists and criminologists, most people who selfishly use Darkpsychology for personal gain have certain behaviors with the term "The DarkTriad."

Dark psychology will assume that any offensive, deviant, or criminal behavior manifesting itself is done for a purpose. They can be seen as wrong or bad, but the other person is doing them for some purpose, and not just because they want to. They will have a reasonable goal most of the time. Someone can abuse to keep their partner in their place to make sure they can get the love and attention they need. Is it something that most societies would do or see as healthy? No, but it's a rational excuse in the mind of the person doing it.

The idea with this is that everyone, even if they know it or not, will have the potential to benefit themselves and their families and victimize other humans and creatures. Some people are more willing to do it than others. For example, you might not think about getting a job promotion or getting someone to notice you, but you might be willing to hurt other people if you knew it would save your life or save someone's life in your family.

While many of us will slow down or hide this type of trend, some will see these impulses and decide to act on them. The idea of dark psychology is to try to understand these perceptions, feelings, thoughts, and even subjective processing systems, which tend to lead to predatory behavior, which is seen as unethical to what most modern society will see as healthy. Or good.

First, we need to take a look at how we can examine and identify the dark side when we observe psychological thinking and behavior. We have to put some kind of measure in place to know what is normal and what is abnormal behavior for humans. The first measure of this will be social norms. Social norms will be one of the actions that society considers reasonable and part of everyday life.

For example, when we look at western culture, it is considered a criminal act to hit another person violently. However, we will give authorizations to harm others to a soldier in the act of war to a police officer in the act of getting a dangerous criminal and to a citizen who is trying to protect his family. Due to the double standards that are here, it is sometimes easy to misinterpret social norms.

The second measure we need to take a look at to measure this is moral. How does a company decide what it sees as wrong and what it sees as right, who has the power to determine this and how laws should be made? Most companies will agree on some of the more significant issues, such as killing is not allowed. But some things are a little more challenging to solve, and companies need to work on it and see what works for them.

The third area of behavior that will come into play will be good manners and what is seen as polite in society. Conduct or conduct consistent with accepted practice such as that of a superior member of a community who knows how to behave in the company of others to establish standards that are seen as a sign of advanced civilization. You might see these as various etiquette standards, such as how to act at the table with a company or to keep the door open for someone else.

Having established societies that have different ways of measuring behavior, through socially acceptable laws, morals, or norms, humans can understand what is allowed and what is not. But even within this, it is possible to manage a wide range of dysfunctional behaviors that will influence others to the point where the person using these behaviors will assume that they are beyond these rules and are allowed to act in any way They would like. And this is where dark psychology and deviant actions will begin to appear.

Understand the dark side of human psychology

There is absolute obscurity observable in the human psyche throughout history. Some would equate it to brutality, crime, and other unwanted aspects of the human condition. Others would say that it is an innate power that all human beings possess, but that not everyone is willing to use in real life. A French saying calledAppel du vide, or the call of emptiness, is used to describe the strange feeling that forces people to think of jumping at high altitudes. Don't believe in the sense that they want to do it, but just a little curious about what would have happened. Seeing that the railings on the second floor of the mall are easy to climb over, the call of emptiness creeps in during the most mundane tasks.

Your instinct is to drain the gas and slow down. If the curve is tight enough, you may also need to brake. But the call of emptiness says, "what would happen if I did nothing and went directly through the security guards? Without a doubt, your car would drive off a cliff if it had enough speed to cross the road. Everyone can remember having at least one version of these thoughts at some point in their lives. People who struggle with mental health may have these thoughts with increasing frequency.

One possible explanation for the call of emptiness is that it is an evolutionary adaptation used to survive. If we can accurately predict dangerous circumstances in advance, then we can also avoid them. And unlike burning your hand on a hot stove, you can't learn to do it by jumping from a tall building. The call of emptiness is remarkable because it shows how much of our psychology is rooted in the survival instinct.

By extension, dark psychology and its practices come from a similar place. It is a primary desire in the human mind to overwhelm, control, and subjugate others. Dark psychology deals mainly with the use of mental tricks and techniques in addition to physical force. Although physical strength, it can be used in combination with other technologies during a dark psychological attack.

Ancient beginnings

Once upon a time, the human race was indistinguishable from the tribal bands of intelligent primates. The society was very simplistic: you lived to eat, reproduce, and take care of your offspring. To achieve these goals, you had to fight against the forces of nature and even fight against your gender. Resources are rare in the desert, making you compete with rival groups. Perhaps this struggle for resources (combined with standard intelligence that favors developments such as cooking food) led to the creation of the smart mind.

The first prehistoric human who noticed that they could grab the end of a stick and use it as a weapon used a form of dark psychology. That is, they used their mental abilities in such a way as to cause another individual harm. This is the physical aspect of dark psychology, which is often overlooked. Dark psychology involves psychological tricks, secret manipulation, and so on. But it also implies projecting one's will against the will of their victims. Sometimes the punches are pulled. Physical alterations, therefore, lead to cycles of abuse.

But what forced that first human to take up a weapon was the struggle for survival.

He understood that the resources would go to the winner and that the winner had the most significant power capabilities. If so, the power would translate to force the infliction. A blunt force weapon is much more efficient than using a bare, hairy punch.

The will to overwhelm or emerge as superior is a common trope in dark psychology. An attacker can create a secret campaign against his victims, without them even knowing it. Usually, it is intended to gain intelligence or to induce the victim to do something. Dark psychological attacks almost always make the victim the main engine, and the attacker remains in the background scene. This not only makes mysterious mental attacks challenging to trace but eliminates aspects of physical strength from the equation. Why is risk hitting someone in the head when you can convince them to give you the resources you are looking for?

This race for superiority is closely related to the development of intelligence. It is not so much brute force that wins in psychological attacks, but the mental cunning of an aggressor. The development of brains with higher functioning in humans has led to many events in the war once you think about it. Yes, there was the invention of agriculture and the great civilizations that followed it, but humanity never seemed to shave the will to power over others.

Intelligence is the human characteristic that allows someone to formulate an exploit against a target. It is what informs our strategies and tactics. An intelligent general seeks the highest ground. Like a wrestler trying to take advantage of his opponent's weight, his armies march into critical positions. This is also a form of dark psychology - tactics designed to cause maximum damage to the enemy.

Someone who lacks physical power can rely on intelligence to compensate for it. A younger brother is weak and weak compared to his older brothers, who mistreat him. But she knows which mother of the drawers keeps the kitchen knives sharp. Intelligence, therefore, is the ability to find a force multiplier as a weapon whenever needed. It is the same story that has been told since the beginning of time.

Only the playing field is slightly different. Physical strength is not necessary, nor desirable when the stakes are not necessarily high. Intensely few people in the modern world are competing for resources or survival, which would require an immediate force multiplier like a weapon. Hugely few people would benefit from aggressive tactics.

But the will to power still exists. Human desires are infinite, and resources (albeit abundant) are still limited to the bottomless hearts of man. Cunning still exists. The desire for control still exists. The need to overwhelm is rooted in the fabric of society. Dark psychology is only the sharp turn on an ancient facet of the human psyche.

The clinical practice of psychology developed at the end of the 19th century and would have been perfected later in the centuries to come. Today it is a vast field encompassing many sub-disciplines, including cognitive and developmental psychology. We now know that the study of the human mind can be treated as a science. It is no longer considered an ambitious attempt to put together unrelated things.

Psychology teaches us that human behavior coincides with developmental and genetic factors. The psychologist John B Watson, famous for his experiments on Albert, once said that if he were given a dozen different children in a controlled environment, he would turn them into specific people. One could be turned into a lawyer, another a doctor, one a beggar, and so on.

Dark psychology teaches us that our behaviors, thoughts, and feelings are exploitable. Just as John B Watson thought he could shape people through controlled experimentation and stimuli, dark psychology users can shape behavior, influence thoughts, and alter feelings. Such a controller or influencer might not be nearly as successful as conditioning a baby from birth. They could, however, use specialized techniques to push someone in the general direction they want them to go.

John B Watson has been widely criticized for his experiments, many of which have fallen under human experimentation violations. His small analyses of Albert, for example, focused on a child subjected to various stimuli in an attempt to create phobias artificially. The aim was to scare little Albert of "hairy" things by introducing him to animals, costumes, and other hairy stuff while making loud and scary noises. John B Watson believed he was able to condition little Albert to fear things he usually wouldn't be. Although some had criticized these claims, little Albert could be afraid of something furry, or was it his association with loud noises that made him afraid? The subject of secret manipulation opens similar criticisms. Are manipulators' actions the main reason a person does something, or is it due to the victim's innate psychology? Whether it is due to one or the other does not matter to the manipulator, as long as the net result is the same. Another famous example of experimental dark psychology that pushed the limits of ethical reasoning at the time was the Stanley Milgram experiment.

Milgram asked the volunteers to come to his laboratory at Yale University, where he would sit behind a control panel in a room.

They designated the role of "teacher." In the next room, there was a person who played the role of "learner." The teacher would ask leaner questions through an intercom system. Whenever the student made a mistake in the problem, the teacher was instructed by the researcher to touch a button on the control panel that would send an electric shock to the student. Unknown to the participants who play the role of teacher, the student was an actor in league with the researcher. Whenever the "electric shock" was "administered," the actor pretended to scream in pain, loud enough to be heard by the teacher. In truth, there were no electric shocks; only the actor played progressively stronger shocks.

At each turn, the researcher pushed the teacher to do his or her job, although this caused another person to experience a physical pain jolt. Every wrong question meant that the teacher had to increase the shock intensity (in volts) on the control panel. And even when the teacher protested not to shock the student again, the researcher was always there to push them to continue the experiment. The final result? An overwhelming majority of the participants administered false, electric shocks that, in real life, would have caused severe physical harm, if not death. The researcher was always there to push them forward to continue the experiment.

The researcher played the role of the manipulator using dark psychological attacks on the teacher. The researcher always wore a white lab coat and reminded the participant how essential their duty was for the experiment. This sense of urgency has been completely fabricated. But since the researcher had a higher social position on the participants (who were ordinary people), they gave the researcher absolute control. All the researchers had to do was make it appear that the participants' behavior was going well and even "essential" for the experiment. But what did that level of importance mean? Just because an authority figure claims that something is important does not mean that the urgency is legitimate. L'

Stanley Milgram's experiment would continue to live in infamy. The research was conducted a few months after the trial against Nazi leaders responsible for war crimes. The similarity between the participants' willingness to administer deadly shocks as compared to Nazi soldiers' desire to carry out atrocities against Jews.

The modern arena

When history is not about life and death, it is about social status, greed, and despair. It is about revenge, small business, and fundamental disagreements. It is also, overall, a story about the psychopathic and sociopathic tendencies of human behavior. It shouldn't be surprising that psychopaths and people like them are natural carriers of dark psychology. These people appear in every social class, from the drug dealer in the city center to the high-powered CEO at the company's highest levels. They could be someone in power like a teacher, a priest, a boss, or a legal guardian. Or just that attractive guy or girl you met at the bar.

There are many reasons for using dark psychology in the modern world. A CEO can use mental games to subvert employees or to convince competitors of profitable deals. A cult leader can do this to gain followers. Or an athlete can use it to soften their rivals before a big game. Most of the time, dark psychology is used to achieve one of three things: influence, money, and power. These are all valuable to the user of dark psychology, but they are difficult to obtain directly. Dark psychology can help a user get what he needs by doing all he can.

Dark psychological attacks are rooted in deception, deception, and manipulation. They are designed to make a person do something, act a certain way, or adopt a series of beliefs without their knowledge of being manipulated. In turn, they become pawns for the politician, the cult leader, or the CEO. Other attacks are aimed at specific targets for specific reasons. A child molester or kidnapper can use dark psychological attacks to trick their victims into thinking that everything is okay. Or that aberrant behavior is suddenly acceptable. This allows the attacker to deal with crimes or other transgressions without the victim being able to do anything about it. It is a state of complete power over another,

Every great cult, political scandal, or mass murder has some aspects of dark psychology for them. In real life, it is as inevitable as it was in the ancient world. After all, we are human. And humans, for whatever reason, like to do things with each other. It should be noted that a specific type of person employs most dark psychological attacks and is a significant minority in the real world.

The prevalence of dark psychology does not mean that everyone you meet is trying to control or cause secret damage. It also does not mean that it is only the madmen and criminals who use dark psychology. Appeals to fear in every day media are a type of mysterious psychological attack. They are targeted messages that try to indulge your deep anxieties to get votes or sell some products. Here the trope of the first is the same: a dark psychological attack is trying to gain influence, power, or money through the victim's submission.

What does this mean for you?

For the average person, the existence of dark psychology does not mean much. We are all bombarded with advertisements and subliminal messages every day to the point that it has normalized in society. Most of us will lead coexisting lives alongside dark psychological attacks that regularly play in the media. Most of these can be safely ignored. The worst-case scenario is that you spend a few hundred dollars on a home surveillance system or voting for a particular politician. It's annoying to deal with, but it doesn't cause any long-term harm.

Few unfortunates, however, will interact daily with that subset of the human population, which is partial in using dark psychology on a whim. These are your psychopaths and sociopaths. To a lesser extent, these are also ordinary people who may have psychopathic or sociopathic tendencies. It is debated whether this type of person was born or created through the products of their environment. It is likely due to a combination of both. People are known to change after enduring difficult circumstances or simply because of the stress of everyday life. In any case, someone in despair could turn to dark psychology very well if he felt he needed it. The most worrying are cases in which mysterious psychological attacks are carried out without the attacker is aware of what he is doing. Sense,

In these cases, it is worth having a superficial knowledge of dark psychology to know how to identify and defend it. There are bad people with bad intentions. Sometimes that evil intent is simply to use you as a pawn to reach an end. For you, it could mean a slight feeling of betrayal or emotional subterfuge. Or, if done by someone close to you, it could mean devastating emotional abuse.

Others try to maximize their profits by any means necessary. Having a deep understanding of human psychology (or just the lack of social customs like a psychopath) allows someone to "hack" the human mind in their favor. There is an entire hacking subfield called social engineering, where an expert hacker can simply call customer service to retrieve confidential information. It is unnecessary to sneak into a computer system to do so if there is a human element that can be targeted.

A skilled social engineer can convince you to do something you shouldn't. No shortage of scams and frauds exist exclusively through social engineering. Some of these can be expensive. Others can even ruin your life, all because you have allowed someone to attack your mind to distract you from the implications.

Dark psychology also exists for those who wish to use it to move forward. Here there is no mystery as to why psychopaths tend towards the top of the social ladder, rather than downward. They tend to do very well economically, socially, and politically. Dark psychology helps them gain influence over others, and slowly they find themselves dealing with people.

Psychopaths are generally more ambitious than the general population, making them excellent leaders.

But for the average boy who wants to understand the darker aspects of human psychology and who wants to both implement and defend dark psychology. One doesn't have to be a psychopath to appreciate the way their minds think. Their way of thinking is unique and translates into the performance as a leader or other position of power. Excellent leadership skills and dark psychology go hand in hand because you always try to find ways to convey your message better or project your will onto others.

Are we the bad guys?

Dark psychology does not mean that it is inherently harmful. Yes, the ability to cause serious harm to others is present but should not be used. Leadership skills, being persuasive, and understanding what moves people can be used for less obscure things. The ethics of dark psychology boils down to what they are used for and in which contexts. Psychological warfare, for example, is a military doctrine designed to harm the enemy or achieve strategic objectives through mental games. A scammer can use dark psychology to perform a scam, and so on. There is no assumption about how dark psychology should be used, only that it can be used.

Chapter 2: Manipulation

Manipulation is a type of social influence in which the goals are to alter others' behavior or perception using techniques, either direct or indirect. Some methods may be considered underhanded; some may not.

Such techniques could be regarded as exploitative and devious by promoting the manipulator's interests, often at another's cost.

Although social influence or impact may represent underhanded manipulation depending on context and motivations, the concept or exercise it is not necessarily negative of social power. Use the necessary tools to your advantage. Ask curious questions, take advantage of time, don't allow yourself to take the blame, and be polite but firm.

Asking questions is an excellent way to take the attention of you back to your manipulator. This can be frustrating for them because they don't expect you to ask your questions, especially if they have already been manipulating you. It's an excellent way to fluster them and make them aware of their own game. They will have to regroup or turn the tables and use another tactic on you, so be aware.

When you are being manipulated or if someone is attempting to get you to do something, you can quickly put them off by saying something along the lines of, "I'll have to think about it." On an everyday basis, your manipulator expects you not to think but do. This can stir them up a bit and confuse them when you don't jump to their demands.

Avoiding people or situations that make you uncomfortable is also another way to deal with manipulation. If you know a person is manipulating, you stay away from them, at least until you can either take control or ignore their tactics. If there are certain places where you feel uncomfortable where there are people who try to get you to do things you don't want to, stay away from that place. It will make life a lot less stressful if you follow your instincts and stay away.

One of the target's most significant issues is taking blame or feeling as if there is something wrong with them. This is manipulator tries to convince you of, then you are one step ahead of them. No matter what they say, you have to take a step back and believe in yourself. Have the positivity that overpowers their negative energy. Allow their remarks and actions to wash over you without allowing them to soak in.

Things to keep in mind about your manipulator:

Most generally, they are just bullies

Usually, a manipulator will back down if you begin to put your foot down. They like passive and compliant people, those easy to control. Once it isn't easy, they will most likely give up.

Often, your manipulator is a victim as well, and this is how they cope. Now that doesn't make it right, but maybe it makes it a little more understanding. Someone who doesn't have any control in their life or is being abused wants to find their power. They search for someone they consider weaker than they are and target them. It makes them feel more robust and less vulnerable.

Other times none of this is the case, and they just are what they are: manipulators through and through. You cannot change them, but you can overpower them and disallow them to control you.

Once you have taken control, you need to set boundaries. Boundaries are essential, especially for people with who you have no choice but to deal regularly. You don't have the luxury of totally taking them out of your life. If this is the case keeping your boundaries and setting consequences for them, crossing the boundaries is essential. This shows them that you are severe and may make them rethink you as a weak individual. But be consistent. Just like a child, if you slip up even once, your manipulator will take that as a free pass and continue to push the limits.What is Manipulation?

Manipulation deals with using your actions, mannerisms, hands, and even other parts of your body to get someone to do what you want or to shape a situation to your desire. You could think of it as selfish, but I tell you that there is a drive-in for every wrongdoing. Therefore, the drive behind manipulation could be positively used. An instance can be seen in how a good DJ tries to bring different music modes together to display his skills in bringing many tunes together into a lovely mix of sounds to the audience. We could say this is almost unfair to the original artist of each song. Also, someone that is good at manipulating would know how to do so in words, emotions, and feelings to the very end of getting his or her main desire.

The practice of manipulation could involve using an indirect scheme and plan to be in charge of relationships. Periodic manipulation consists of telling a friend that they are looking well when they are mentally depressed or/and physically down. This is quite technical as it will affect your friend's perceptions of you, which will eventually translate to how the person relates to you. Emotional abuse can be associated with manipulation, especially when it is experienced in very close relationships. Depending on the point of view, someone can consider manipulation negative when the person being manipulated is affected physically, emotionally, or mentally. In contrast, another person can argue that conducting help to put one's surroundings and environment, including people, into subjection and under control. Moreover, manipulators could find it hard to connect with their original selves, and being manipulated can lead to ill effects in an individual.

To understand manipulation, you have to identify the significant three distinct types. First, we have manipulation of options in which rewards or threats modify the environment's options. The second one is the manipulation of information; here, the individual's way of perceiving things is adjusted. The understanding of the situation gets affected. Also, psychological manipulation is a process of influencing someone such that there is a change in mental cognition.

During manipulative encounters, there are four main components of manipulations: the hearer, motive, covertness, and interest of the speaker. These are usually referred to as prerequisites to manipulation. Any form of manipulation is geared towards affecting a hearer or victim. The target often will behave in such a way to oppose how he acts before being manipulated. In a manipulative situation, the manipulator has a broader vision spectrum, which means that the manipulator knows much better than the target.

Talking about motive, is this not what characterizes manipulation itself? The intention of the speaker determines to what extent the target is manipulated.

However, this intention cannot be known to the hearer else; it would be self-defeating. There is usually a communication involving the hearer, the speaker, and the speaker's communicated motives.

For the widespread view on manipulation to hold, it then needs to remain covert. To a large extent, I can assume that the speaker's motive is a critical feature in manipulation. It is designed to suit the desire and interest of the speaker. I can also tell you that there is a correlation between a manipulative mechanism and the manipulator's motive.

It is imperative to know that manipulations can be done unconsciously or without being aware, while some people manipulate deliberately. Intentional manipulators are tricky. They would even brag about what they do because they are very much aware. The game known as manipulation enables manipulators to be wise, smart, and cunny at the same time. They are also self-centered, so you cannot claim to be good at manipulating and care for others.

Various Forms of Manipulation

Unintentional resistance to others' demands can be making excuses, blaming others, sarcasm, hiding anger, among others.

Indirect or Implied Threats. An example of this is when, as a mother, you give your child a bad look for dropping his or her dirty uniform on the floor.

Deceitfulness in character or behavior includes cheating, fabrication, corruption, and even stealing.

Selfishness in disseminating useful information. For example, you have a friend that needs a job as you are, and where you get information about companies having vacancies, you hold it back from him or her.

She is making someone leave a company or association of loved ones. A single mother could fall into this category, where because of hatred from the child's father, she isolates the child from the father and his family, who truly loves him.

Attempt to destabilize someone's belief. This often leads to misdirection, denial, and low self-esteem.

Forcefully criticizing, insulting, or denouncing another person. A typical example is bullying

It is achieving a goal via sexual intercourse. This is common among employers and employees.

However, if manipulation is not being addressed, people who are being manipulated can suffer from poor mental health. Chronic manipulation could result in depression, anxiety, wrong coping methods, lying, and difficulty trusting people. It could also make a victim lose his or her value system and doubt things in their real sense. An instance was illustrated in a classic movie titled Gaslight. In a subtle manner, the husband of a woman manipulated her until she no longer depends on how she perceives things. The man secretly turned down the gaslights, and he made his wife believe that the way the light looks dim was all in her head.

Manipulators are also good at saying sweet things their victims would like, and most words from them are not all that true. They take advantage of being skilled in this to develop a close and fantastic connection with people. A manipulator will deliberately create an imbalanced way of using a victim to their advantage. Until such a person gets what he/she wants, they can go to any length.

There is some subtle behavior that you should smell manipulation when you sense them either from you or others. Instances include acting dumb and pretending to be friendly and lovely all the time. If we all what to be truthful, at a point or the other in our lives, we have been manipulative. Sometimes, to control people, tell a lie to get out of a situation, or even flatter. To some people, it is a way of life.

As you know, or have even experienced, manipulators are everywhere and around us. The question should be, what personalities do they possess? A manipulator could be your next-door friend who spreads gist and gossip about you. They could even be your family members who make people around them feel insecure or who always create chaos, so in the end, anybody could manipulate you. On the road, manipulators are usually criminals who rely on gimmicks to distract you from taking your belongings.

Common Traits

Use of Language

We have shown how powerful language can be an excellent tool for persuasion. There is more to the manipulative controller, though, than mere words. They will use tactics that mislead and unbalance their target's inner thoughts. We now understand that through language, they will:

Use mistruths to mislead and confuse their target's regular thinking pattern.

Force their target to decide the speed, so they don't have time to analyze and think.

Overwhelmingly talk to their target, making them feel small.

Criticize their target's judgment, so they begin to lose their self-esteem.

Raise the tone of their voice and not be afraid to use aggressive body language.

Ignore their target's needs. They are only interested in getting what they want and at any cost.

Invasion of Personal Space

Most of us set boundaries around ourselves without realizing we are doing so. It is a kind of unspoken rule to protect our private space, such as not sitting so close that you are touching another person, especially a stranger. A manipulative character cares nothing about overstepping such boundaries. Whether this is because they do not understand or they do not care is unclear. Initially, they are unlikely to invade their target's personal space. They will seek to build up a good rapport first. This shows that they understand boundaries because once they gain the confidence of their target, they will then ignore them.

Fodder for Thought

Manipulators tend to be very selfish, with limited social skills. Their only concern is for themselves. Everything they do in life will be concerning how it affects them, not how their actions affect others. Does this mean that they have a psychopathic disorder?

Take empathy, for instance. Controlling manipulators are unlikely ever to show kindness. The heart is a natural human emotion that aids in our survival techniques. A study by Meffert et al. indicates that those with a psychopathic disorder can control empathetic emotions (4c). They lack sympathy of any kind because another weakness is simply another tool for them. When they detect any fault in their target's resolve or personality, they will exploit it. The consequences to their victim are of little importance. The targets weakness's feed the manipulator's strength, making them bolder and often crueler in their actions.

Creating Rivalry

Another tactic of the controlling manipulator is backstabbing. They may tell you how great a person you are to your face, making themselves look good. Behind your back, they are busy spreading malicious gossip and untruths about you. This is a classic trait of a controlling manipulator as it creates a rivalry between people. Then, they can pick sides that will make them look favorable, particularly to their target. It can act as the first stage of getting close to their target. Once bonded, they can start to build up trust, making it easier to manipulate the target in the future. If you recognize a backstabber, keep them at a distance. Their plan is selfish, so it is better not to let them into your personal life. There is no point in treating them as they treat you in revenge. It will turn out to be exhausting, playing them at their own game. If they know that you are on to them, they may attempt to lure you back with praise; remember that it is false.

Domineering Personality

It is unlikely that a manipulative person will outwardly show any form of weakness. An essential part of their facade is to show conviction about their views. They seek to impress, believing they are right about everything. Almost to the point that if they realize they are wrong, they will still argue that they are right. On a one-to-one level, that invariably means that your position is always wrong. As they will chip away at your beliefs, they seek to undermine your sense of self-esteem. Once they have achieved this, then there is no holding them back. They seek to domineer others, often speaking with a condescending tone to belittle their victims. Using ridicule is yet another tool against their target, merely because it will make themselves look better. If you ridicule them back, they will seek to turn the tables, accusing you of being oversensitive to their "joke." The kind of joke that only the teller sees the funny side.

Passive Aggressive Behavior

A common trait of many hard-core manipulators is passive-aggressive behavior. Because they prefer to be popular, they do not wish to be seen as doing anything wrong. Not that a manipulator would ever admit to doing anything wrong. They are experts with facial expressions that are meant to dominate and intimidate. This may include; knitting eyebrows, grinding teeth, and rolling eyes. It may also include noises such as tutting and grunting sounds. It is a prevalent behavior for such a character, as little anyone else has to say that they will agree upon. For most manipulators, it is their life's ambition to show people up by proving them wrong.

This ranges from the aggressive look, where they seek to stare their target down. Or, It could be in response to their disagreement on something their target said. They may smirk and shake their head, turn their back, anything to show their strong disapproval. It is all a ploy to make themselves look superior and put others down.

Moody Blues

What of the emotional stability of the manipulator? Is it that which makes them behave the way they do? Do they even know what happiness is? The answer to that is a most definite yes, at least to the latter.

Happiness is a tool used initially to help them manipulate. A happy target is more likely to comply. This, in itself, makes the manipulator happy, or at least in the sense of what they consider happiness. But their joyfulness is a perverted model of what most others think pleasure to be. Their satisfaction was built on the foundations of another's misery. A misery that they have caused with their cruel manipulations. Equally, though, a manipulator is prone to mood swings. Most likely to happen when things are not going to plan. One minute they are euphoric at their latest conquest. Then next, they could be deflated entirely at their failure to succeed. One thing is sure for those who live with or become a target of this type of authoritarian character, they will be unhappy all the time.

Intimidation

One aspect of manipulation, often used as a last resort, is intimidation and bullying. When everything else has failed, they begin to use threats to get their way. Some, though, may use pressure from the onset. It may in a source of authority. For example, let's take the role of a manipulative boss. You have requested a day off. They don't want to allow you your request but have no choice. It is your right. This type of person would like their pound of flesh first. They will set goals for you to reach to delay or cancel your request, such as moving project deadlines forward. This way, they have their little victory over you.

Alternatively, such a manipulator may use the tactic of the silent treatment. Ignoring someone to the point that it becomes apparent you have displeased them. They seek to make you feel the guilty party.

Other more direct intimidating actions may include stance. Using their height or build to tower over you, or standing uncomfortably close.

Be careful as they will seek revenge for wrongdoings they perceive done to them. Nothing will go unnoticed under their watchful eye. Everyone is a potential target. But, the weak are more likely to walk into their traps because they are the ones who are more comfortable to dominate. The vulnerable will have little resistance and are easier to bully and coerce. Many of these traits seem more fitting to men, but women can be cruelly manipulative too.

This is a person who will never back down in an argument. Never admit they are wrong. Never apologize for anything. A manipulator will never show respect but will expect everyone else to show them respect.

They love nothing more than to embarrass others. Playing the dumb one is common practice, just to force another person to explain themselves further. At every opportunity, the manipulator will jump in with some sarcastic remark, "hurry up, we're all waiting for your intellectual explanation," or "why has no one else ever heard of this?" Their sole aim is to make the other person look a fool, but without seeming to be the one who made it happen. Oh no, the victim did that to themselves because they are stupid.

Behavioral Traits of Favorite Victims of Manipulators

Sensitive people

Power is a component of manipulation, but not the only element. Intelligent and sensitive people have control, but they do not use it to manipulate others. The person who does the manipulation is the one that has greater comparative power and is unable to get what he wants in mutual agreement or thought other means and rests to an underhanded tactic, which usually results in manipulation.

To neutralize the emotional manipulation, you have to stop caring what the other person says or feels. This balances the power they have over you. Power to compel action using external force is not emotional manipulation – and if you believe that physical harm may result from a denial of a request by the aggressor, you have a problem more significant than emotional manipulation and beyond the scope of the topic. But the power to compel you from within you is emotional manipulation. That gives you two alternatives. First, it can weaken you out or make you realize that you have the ultimate power over what goes on inside. Don't let anyone on the outside dictate what goes on inside.

Ultimately only you have the power of your destiny, and you need to make it a habit to remember that.

Emphatic people

An empath is someone who absorbs more emotion than a typical person. If they can sense tremendously more than anyone else, then the slight detection the other person would like you to do something for them will be magnified, and they would go about doing it just so as not to feel bad about it. This does not mean the other person has power over the empath.

It is more prevalent that women are more empathic and the softer side of the equation. Nothing wrong with that, but when you remind someone that that is who they are, they take on the stereotypes, and then they become easier to manipulate.

Being told that you are beautiful, sexy, gorgeous are all ways that lead to a specific form of weakening of your intellect, and those results in the path to manipulation. Well, not all times, but it can be. Men tend to pay obsequious complements to women so that they can take advantage of the situation. It is not the complement that breaks them, but the reminder that they are women in conjunction with the supplement.

Your frame of mind needs to be strengthened before the event. It's like building the walls to a medieval city. You don't erect the barriers just when the marauding armies arrive. You make them ahead of time.

The other thing you have to do is alter the stereotype you have of your gender and yourself. Once you neutralize that, it's harder for anyone to use that to get you to submit. If you look at the art of enslaving people, a few slave owners can control hundreds of slaves even today. Why? Can't the slaves overpower them with numbers? No, because their frame of mind has been manipulated and their mind has submitted,

Protect your mind and thoughts, and you will be able to fend off a large part of the manipulating aggressor.

Fear of loneliness

A victim who seems lonely, seeking support, comfort, and desperation is more likely to be love-bombed and at a higher intensity than others. If the victim is more grounded, they will need a less intense, and maybe more subtle, way in the love bombing.

The idea behind working with love bombing is that it will create an intense feeling of affection, trust, and compliance from the victim over to their manipulator. The extent to which love bombing will be used and the person it is used on will often depend on how the manipulator assesses the situation.

Fear of disappointing others

Suppose your insecurities are triggering you to believe negative thoughts, which will materialize into unfavorable activities. In that case, that's when your partnership can begin feeling several of the adverse effects of your insecurity. It might not take place overnight, yet understand that it's OK if you require to overcome some insecurities, whether that's on your very own, with a therapist, or with the love and support of your companion. Below are seven signs that your instabilities are influencing your connection, according to professionals.

Instability comes from our concern of 'not having sufficient' or 'not being enough.' These anxieties are vanity based. When we are unconfident, we bother with what others think about us and do not have a strong feeling of self and even healthy self-worth. Here are a couple of indications of instability that can indicate you need to lock out the ego's voice and be true to on your own.

1. Flaunting

One of the most usual instability indicators is boasting regarding what you have and what you have attained. Troubled individuals possess of trying to thrill other individuals. They then end up being hopeless for recognition from the world's exterior. Nonetheless, if you have a protected sense of self, you don't feel the requirement to excite others regularly and certainly do not need other people to validate you.

2. Regulating

Individuals who are monitoring can occasionally appear to be stable. Nevertheless, controlling behavior originates from anxiety and also insecurity. It is just one of the most common indications of instability. When we are afraid that we may not be able to deal with what life tosses at us, we attempt frantically to regulate the globe around us and maintain it within appropriate boundaries so that we feel risk-free and safely secure. This can lead us to control other people as we can feel safe if they act in foreseeable ways. When we understand that we can handle life, whatever happens, we no more feel the demand to regulate every little thing to feel secure rigidly. After that, we can start to go with the flow and delight in life in all its messy glory.

3. Stress and anxiety

Anxiety often originates from a sensation of not being good enough, as well. Frequently when we are anxious, we are afraid of what other people may think of us, or we are so scared we will ruin in some way. Individuals that are protected in themselves don't feel anxious about points a lot. This is since they do not put so much emphasis on being right regularly. Although they might still establish high requirements for themselves, they do not defeat themselves for every regarded mistake. They approve that they are only human, which they will often obtain things wrong, and that's okay.

4. Individuals pleasing

A clear sign of instability is the demand to please other individuals at all times. This hinders living your very own life. It can occasionally seem like your life does not belong to you when you are regularly attempting to make others happy. People with high self-esteem show caring and empathy for others but do not feel they are accountable for others' happiness. And that is real. You are exempt from other individuals' satisfaction, and you do not require to secure or rescue them from every unpleasant thing they might experience.

If you are a people pleaser, you must make room in your life for you. You must obtain the possibility to do the things that make you happy and follow your very own desires and not merely assist others in accomplishing theirs. However, people-pleasing can result in bitterness and even a feeling of martyrdom. This is not a healthy and balanced method to be. People-pleasing is terrible for you and is likewise bad for others as it is often harmful to their growth, too.

5. Perfectionism

If you seem like nothing you do is good enough or spend an excessive amount of time obtaining points 'perfect,' then this may signify insecurity. This typically boils down to a fear of failure or criticism. You find it tough to let go and proceed from a job since you fear the outcome may not be what you hoped. Regrettably, this can result in you obtaining stuck, never finishing things, or investing much too lengthy on whatever you do. This can suggest you stop working to meet due dates or let people down. This harms your self-esteem and also can be a descending spiral. Perfectionism can be tough to escape from, but once again, having a healthy and balanced feeling of self and being kinder and more accepting of that you are is the place to start.

6. Anxiety

Feelings of anxiety can often signify insecurity. Clinical depression can happen when a buildup of tension triggers you to pull back from life. Stress commonly makes us take out of the world to ensure that we won't get injured or criticized or won't fall short. By developing a strong feeling of self, you can venture out right into the world without a lot of anxiety and also anxiety. Of course, stress is not always straightforward to recoup from; however, beginning with small acts of self-care and being mild on your own is an excellent way to start to move out of crippling clinical depression.

Chapter 3: The Make-Up Of A Manipulator

Psychological manipulation is the exploitation of other people's emotions and vulnerabilities. People generally know how to protect themselves from physical attacks, but manipulators strike at their targets psychological and emotional weaknesses.

Humans are more vulnerable than we care to admit but we also have unconscious ways of protecting ourselves. This self-protection is mostly achieved through developing a positive mindset, healthy boundaries, resilience, patience, a strong character and learning to stand up for ourselves. However, these natural defenses become relaxed around the people we believe have our best interests at heart. Also, if we're going through an emotionally difficult time such as a divorce, illness, loss of job or death of a loved one, then we become much more vulnerable and open to being taken advantage of. This becomes one of the keys of successful manipulation - finding a weak point or moment of vulnerability in the target and then exploiting it.

The Art of Manipulation

Manipulation dictionary definition -

'the action of manipulating something in a skillful manner'.

'the action of manipulating someone in a clever or unscrupulous way'.

From these dictionary explanations, we see the main points are the use of the words 'skilful', and 'clever'. These words highlight the fact that Manipulation involves a certain degree of intelligence and ability. The word 'unscrupulous' points to the fact that it's something underhand or deceitful.

This is how we generally understand Manipulation; as something negative, harmful or bad. But what if you could learn how to use it to create a better life? Earn more money? Attract your dream partner? Surely it wouldn't seem so evil then?

My understanding of Manipulation is as a subtle technique of getting what we want from others willingly, even if it's something they may not normally consent to.

No one likes to feel they've been manipulated or taken advantage of, still, we all occasionally manipulate one another. At the same time, we also find it acceptable to be manipulated in certain situations, such as by politicians or salespeople for instance. We may not openly admit it but deep down we know when we've been taken advantage of. But due to evolutionary programming, most of us will generally look to see the good in others. We think to ourselves, 'of course, other people have our best interests at heart', 'of course, this salesperson wants us to buy this car because it's the best choice for us and not because he has a monthly sales quota to achieve'.

Some of us are quick to point the finger at those who use persuasion tactics to get what they want and even label them manipulators. But, then we read about the politicians who promise people one thing to get their vote, but then backtrack once they're in power and nothing much ever gets said about it. Such people don't experience the same sort of backlash for the methods they use to get what they want as Joe Bloggs in your office does.

I point this out not because manipulation occurs more often than we care to realize but because learning these skills can make us better communicators while also teachings us how to protect ourselves against been manipulated.

Skilled Manipulators

Manipulators differ in skill, ruthlessness and the methods they use. But what they all have in common is the ability to penetrate the psychology of others.

Skilled manipulators not only know how to spot psychological weaknesses or the secret ambitions of those they target, but they also know how to use these insights to stir people into action so that they can gain something.

This subtle art involves being able to play with people's feelings and weaknesses in such a way that they often don't understand what's happening until it's too late. Manipulators develop such a mindset, that the moment they get into a new situation, whether socially or professionally, they immediately start assessing people for their value, usability, and vulnerabilities. Once a 'suitable' individual is identified, the manipulator will start analyzing their body language, facial impressions, mannerisms, vocabulary and any other subtle signs – which all lead to an assessment of the personality and character of the individual. After they've narrowed down their choice of whom to focus on, they'll work to create a relationship or closer bond. They analyze their victims until they know what makes them tick and when their victim trusts them enough to gladly accept their suggestions, they then go for the jugular.

The general tactic is to appear likable, trustworthy and friendly, usually by showing a high degree of empathy and understanding. When we show interest in people, it naturally lowers their defenses.

Kin Hubbard describes this stage very well, 'The fellow that agrees with everything you say is either a fool or he is getting ready to skin you'.

Exploiting Others' Vulnerabilities

Many of us can feel vulnerable for any number of reasons – a lack of resources, disadvantaged social status, physical disabilities, language barriers, culture and so on. In a work setting, we may find ourselves vulnerable if we're new, less experienced or less educated than others. In a social environment, one can be left feeling exposed because of their economic status, their family or educational background. In interpersonal relationships, one can be vulnerable if they come from a different culture or background, or if they have a physical disability, or maybe a less accepted sexual or religious orientation. In some cultures, unmarried or divorced women are vulnerable.

The key difference between skilled manipulation and the more extreme methods, such as brainwashing, blackmailing, bribery or racketeering, is that manipulators have a 'softer' approach and don't openly confront their victims with aggressive threats or excessive demands. This is what makes them so deadly. It's easy to protect yourself when you know who the enemy is, but in the case of manipulation, the offender is often a friend or someone you thought you could trust. This makes it easier for the victim to be lead into some falsehood.

Some people unknowingly attract manipulators, acting almost as a magnet. These are usually very naive, neurotic or insecure individuals. This is not to judge such people but with them, flattery, guilt or shame games can usually yield quick results.

Basic Manipulative Behaviors

1 - Using Your Words against you

This is a common method used by most people not just manipulators. It is also an incredibly powerful sales technique. By simply asking someone the right questions, we can gain a golden nugget of information which can then be used against them at a later point. In the case of a sales negotiation, a salesman may have uncovered your real motive behind making a purchase, this might be that you need a new car so you can travel to see your family on weekends. Once the salesperson knows your real buying motive, he can literally beat you to death with it until you agree to the sale. It can be difficult to argue against something which is true, which is why arguments are best won if we use reasons people give us against them. We could say 'you said this......', or 'you did this...', by repeatedly highlighting the other person's actual behavior or words it traps them from overcoming our side of the argument.

2 - Refuse to be held accountable

Manipulators may simply lie and twist truths when it suits them to get out of disagreements or arguments. But their skill lies in the level of conviction they use to spin these lies. They tell these untruths in such a way they actually believe what they're saying.

3 - Blame

Emotional manipulators will try to move away from taking responsibility for a mistake. Rather they'll look to shift the blame onto a susceptible or weaker person. They may often play the victim card to make other people feel guilty. If they want to gain something from you, they may try to make you feel sympathy for their plight so you justify to yourself your reasons for helping or supporting them.

Exploiting people comes easier to some than to others. Successful manipulators often don't feel sorry for the pain they may be causing their victim. Their greatest asset, which is usually a high degree of empathy, also becomes their greatest weapon.

4 - Emotional Detachment

Emotional detachment can be a highly desirable skill for a manipulator. It sometimes stems from psychological trauma usually in childhood. This is often called emotional numbing, dissociation or emotional blunting and is considered 'unhealthy' since it is a complete disconnection from the emotions. It develops as a result of childhood trauma to help the child avoid feeling painful or hurtful emotions. Unfortunately, when these children grow up into adults they often bring this programming with them.

Those who are natural manipulators probably have been subjected to such trauma which has lead to a numbing of their emotions and feelings.

Basic Manipulation Techniques

We're all guilty of playing tricks on others from time to time but they're usually quite harmless. Most of these would fall under the category of 'Basic' manipulation skills.

Whereas a higher skilled manipulator would use more advanced methods to covertly influence. We tend to use less sophisticated methods in our everyday lives to get our needs met. Most of the time we're not even aware we're being manipulative.

There are many ways in which people can be coerced or forced into doing things they don't want to do, the most common methods include: guilt tripping, complaining, lying, denying, feigning ignorance or innocence, blaming, bribery, undermining, mind games, emotional blackmail, evasiveness, fake concern, apologies, flattery, gifts, and favors – as you can see that's a long list. If we're honest with ourselves, most of us have used a few of these methods more than once. This isn't to suggest we're evil or sinister people but just shows how common these methods.

Lines such as, 'After all I've done for you...', or 'If your parents ever found out about this...', or 'There's no one in the office who could do this as well as you....', are just some of the most common phrases used to make someone feel guilty or obliged to do what is asked.

Here we will consider some basic strategies which are easy to learn and apply.

Basic influential Techniques

Get your ideas into someone else's head

Make the target feel relaxed in your company. People are easily influenced when they're in an alpha state of mind, being calm and quiet promotes this state.

By paying close attention to your words and tonality you can lure people into relaxed states more easily. Observe if your words and tonality are having the desired effect on your targets physiology, posture and body language. Practice this with close relatives and friends, notice how they naturally relax or become excited based on how you communicate with them. Raising the voice or speaking quickly naturally gets people more alert, whereas speaking slower and quietly tends to have a more relaxing effect. Also pay attention to people's eyes, here we can usually see the first signs relaxation as the pupils naturally dilate and get larger.

You can pay even closer attention by looking to see if the pulse in the neck is beating fast or slow. This requires practice, but it can further help determine how the opposite party is feeling.

Breathing patterns also change in relation to the state of mind of an individual. When we are relaxed we tend to breath more deeply otherwise known as 'belly breathing' but when overwhelmed or stressed the breathing tends to be shallower.

If you can get someone feeling relaxed (large pupils), calm (breathing slowly and deeply) and safe in your company (open body posture), this is when they'll be most susceptible to your influence.

Use Hot Words

'Hot words' effectively bring out emotions in people. They are most often used in sales and politics; however, they can also be successfully used in everyday conversations to influence or persuade.

These words may seem ordinary at first, but they're actually very suggestive because of their connection to the senses, words such as - hear this, see that, feel free, imagine etc. The power of such words can instantly invoke a certain state of mind through psychological short-circuiting.

By listening carefully to someone, try to figure out which hot words would have the biggest impact on them. For example, if someone often uses phrases such as "I really don't see where the problem is" or "I don't see the purpose of...". These are visual learners who's thought process is based on what they can envision (see). You can best reach visual types by using phrases such as "See it this way...", or "Look at it from another angle".

On the other hand, if someone speaks in a way such as, "I feel they were wrong..." or "I feel lost". These are kinesthetic learners and understand things best through feeling. With these types, use words such as "I feel I know what you should do", or "Feel free to call me anytime...".

The other most common learning type is auditory. Listen out for people who speak using phrases such as "I like the sound of that" or "listen to your gut".

Here you're simply adapting your language and communication to match the way others are interpreting the world. This means your message is more likely to be received in the way it was intended.

But regardless of personality type, some words just hold more power than others. Salesmen and journalists are masters of communication and know how to use the right words at the right time, for instance, the word 'cash' is more powerful than the word 'money, 'beaten' is more powerful than 'assaulted', 'starving' is more powerful than 'hungry' and so on.

Humans naturally shift through information which doesn't at first appeal to them. Hot words invoke feelings, stir up emotions and create related images and thoughts in the mind. When used skillfully, they can influence a person's decisions often without you even having to suggest anything. By learning about your target, you get to understand what to say and how to say it to get a response.

8 basic steps to developing manipulation skills

➢ Learn to read people. Make judgments about people and then see if you're right.

➢ Have a pleasant appearance. Always try to look, well-groomed, clean and tidy.

➢ Adopt pleasant manners. Be polite, helpful, courteous and kind.

➢ Act friendly, or at least try to look friendly.

➢ Show concern, care, empathy, be a shoulder to cry on.

➢ Be organized. To plan a manipulation tactic, benign or complicated, you must be able to plan accordingly from A to Z, sometimes even changing tactics.

➢ Develop patience. Things don't always go according to plan.

➢ Additional qualities: ruthlessness, cunningness, emotional detachment, shrewdness.

The art of manipulation involves two main aspects: concealing your real intentions and knowing the vulnerabilities of the target.

Chapter 4: Effects Of Dark Psychology

Given the little we now understand dark psychology, we realize that some of the more shocking criminal offenses are rooted in certain dark psychology-related personality traits. That is, though, a larger side effect. Why does this deep psychology influence us if it influences us? I can tell you there are no "ifs" to this question, and I'll explain it in a few moments.

The attacker and victim are experiencing the effects of the dark mind. We must explore some elements of dark psychology to learn the impacts. People who display characteristics deemed enigmatic such as narcissism, psychopathy, and Machiavellianism, are likely to encounter problems in certain facets of their relationships. When these three characteristics are present in one individual, they are more likely to commit a crime. The three foregoing personality attributes have different features clustered within them.

For instance, narcissism is characterized by a sense of entitlement, feelings of superiority, deep-seated envy of others' achievements, and exploitative behavior. Psychopathy has an absence of conscience, an absence of remorse, destructive impulsive behavior, ego-centeredness, and an unwillingness to take responsibility. Machiavellian features are signs of selfishness, ruthlessness, and cynical behavior. These traits are separately problematic, but they may spell trouble when together, especially in the relation between an individual and others. For instance, in the workforce, the person may exhibit the following:

Underperform even the most mundane tasks

Disrupt the workflow because they are unable to get along with others

Other people will intensely dislike him

Their impulsivity will lead them to make questionable, non-ethical decisions

They are more likely to commit a white-collar crime if they are put in an administrative capacity.

But it is not just their working relationships that are struggling. In their relationships, they will experience the following problems:

A constant need for attention and validation for a partner can be exhausting, leading to faster expiration dates on relationships

To exploit their partners, they resort to physical and emotional blackmail

They tend to be either verbally, emotionally, or physically abusive.

People in relationships with them are paying a high emotional cost. If, for the sake of your health and general well-being, you have encountered a person whose relationships are characterized by such experiences, steer clear of them. If, on the other side, you are the one experiencing this, search out the psychological help you need to change. You must change your attitude and experience in the correct form of therapy, no matter how deep-rooted such issues are. The first step is to accept the issue, understand that you have a concern, and promptly pursue help.

It leaves us emotionally and mentally drained to deal with individuals who have the traits I mentioned above to the rest of us. The effect may be painful at times and fatal in extreme cases.

The biggest impact dark psychology has on anyone is that it has a strong sense of loss. We're losing our valuables, we're losing relationships, we're losing ourselves, and we're sacrificing our lives with others. It is extremely unfortunate. Considering all, it's fair to assume the effect of this darkness is profound.

According to experts, if a person exhibits one of the dark personality traits, there is a very high probability that the individual will exhibit the others. In general society, if larger segments of the community displayed such traits, it is fair to assume that there would be extremely elevated crime levels within our culture. This is not to suggest that citizens who reside in towns or countries with elevated criminals are more geared towards criminality. Other factors lead to concern. However, the possibility cannot be entirely ruled out either.

The ripple effect in actions directly related to, and as a consequence of, dark personality characteristics is one factor that cannot be phased entirely. Other negative habits transform offenders into abusers as well. That process persists far into the future before someone has the strength to take the brave step and break away. For starters, more frequently than not, children from abusive homes grow up to be abusers. In certain cases, they find themselves stuck in similarly dysfunctional marriages to break free from a parental mold even though they are not the perpetrators themselves. It is like feeling a really heavy gravitational pull against the aggressive elements that dominated their home throughout their youth.

For others, being victims may have such a tremendous impact on their psychology that it forces everything to crack within them, causing them to snap. They lose all control of their innate instincts in a fleeting moment and function solely upon the greatest emotion that emerges — typically, rage. This disorder is what allows some people to plead temporary insanity. Yet some people accept the dark feelings as they 'snap.' Any truth concept goes out the window. The effects of this are typically catastrophic.

Chapter 5: Stop The Manipulators

Many manipulators will do their best to make sure that the victim doesn't realize what's happening but there are ways to use this to your advantage.

By creating stakes, the manipulator has control over you because they know that either way they win. During those stakes, it's important to recognize that they don't expect you do not play their game.

A manipulator knows how to use dark psychology to make the victim do what they ask. If they are constantly picking on you or making note of every mistake you've ever made, the manipulator is planning to use this against. Their reactions to the things that disappoint them are important too.

Pay attention to how they respond to you in the beginning because this will change as time passes. The manipulator will take note of how you react to things not going your way. If you are prone to fits of rage yourself when frustrated, the manipulator will know how to use that against you. If you get depressed or are deeply saddened by failure, the manipulator will use that against you. Dark psychology focuses on human reaction to situations and using that to influence a situation.

A manipulator will focus on every reaction, every moment of joy, sadness or anger and twist it to suit their needs. For example, Liam and Cierra are brother and sister. Liam wants Cierra to stay home from summer camp this year because he doesn't want her to ruin his summer. Liam knows that Cierra doesn't like Sarah D. from her grade and would do anything to avoid her. Liam tells Cierra that this year Sarah is going to be at the summer camp and she's going to be bunking in her cabin. Cierra not wanting to spend a whole summer sleeping in the same room as Sarah drops out of the summer camp and now Liam gets to go alone like he wanted. Something as simple as knowing that his sister didn't like another student was all he needed to manipulate her into doing what he wanted.

It's easy to manipulate someone into doing what you ask when you know what grinds their gears. Using dark psychology could make it easier for a manipulator to take advantage, and the victim wouldn't know how they allowed them to use these weaknesses.

Narcissistically they would believe they are smarter than their victim and pay close attention to how they react to even the manipulator themselves. Manipulators love over sharers, or people who don't care who knows about their lives. These people are easier to manipulate because they lay everything about them on the table.

For example, Tyra is always talking about her bad marriage to John, John's friend that wants to have sex with Tyra knows how bad his marriage to his wife is and knows how John acts. Hence, he portrays the exact opposite of that and manipulates Tyra into sleeping with him by complaining about his friendship with John.

A manipulator will always make things go their way by using keywords that may trigger a response out of the victim. They may berate them constantly for something small or make them feel guilty for having any reaction to what's happening around them at all. A manipulator's main tool to anything is pulling the wool over the victim's eyes. Dark persuasion is making the victim feel like they have no control over the situation or giving all the "power" to the victim. Prolonging events or constant empty promises may occur.

The manipulator will always show that they are in complete control but it's up to the victim to say they aren't falling for it. They will find ways to make it feel like the victim has the power of choice, but the manipulator has carefully thought out every step from the moment they picked their victim.

Dark persuasion considers age, creed, upbringing, religion and/or sexuality. The manipulator will take all these factors and create a trap for their victim. The victim would be completely unaware of what's happening, but they will feel like the events are correlating with their behavior or with what's happening as the situation transpires.

They won't be able to see how the manipulator has taken control of what's happening and leads them to doing what they ask of them without much question. The manipulator is skilled at masking their true intentions of what they are doing, and the victim won't see they are being manipulated.

For example, Marie wants Donny to pay for her to go to Miami. She knows that Donny never got to travel because of his parents not being able to afford it, so she makes him feel bad that she can't afford it. Donny doesn't realize that she is doing this just get her way and agrees to pay for the trip. Marie has known Donny for a few months and knew that from conversations they had together that something like that would work.

When unmasking the true intentions of another person, you must consider the person that you are dealing with. Sometimes you feel like they are manipulating the situation and when you feel that way, it's good to step up. However, if you can't identify the manipulation, one way is to focus on the person's choice of words.

If they are constantly repeating something or constantly return to one specific phrase in a spiral during a conflict, they are concentrating the focus on what they want. Look out for how they react to simple requests, something simple can become a chore for someone that is trying to manipulate a situation and they will use these repeated words or actions to get a rise of out the victim.

For example, Duncan doesn't want to do the dishes, so he complains to his sister about how he must do dishes all the time at work and that he gets cuts on his hands whenever he does them from the silverware and cutlery. Every time he doesn't want to do dishes, this is what Duncan will say and his sister will do it because she doesn't want her brother to suffer.

However, once she noticed that he only does this when he must do them, she eventually told him that she is no longer doing it. Once you recognize that you are being manipulated, it's easier to prevent it from continuing.

Manipulators may also get angry over very little things, to make themselves look and feel bigger. They will start fights over someone not listening to them or they will start a fight over the way a person looks at them.

A manipulator will shout especially when they know they are in the wrong and don't want to admit it. As mentioned, if they feel cornered or don't know how to make themselves look like the victim, shouting is the next method. If someone for no reason just explodes the fear they incite can make someone do what they want.

For example, Lorne wants Greg to stop asking him about why he came home late from work. Greg accuses him of cheating, Lorne tosses his coat down onto the floor and starts shouting at Greg for yelling at him when he's tired and has been working. Greg backs down because he is afraid of what would happen if he continued to yell at Lorne. And Lorne knew that Greg would if he yelled at him because Greg came from an abusive household. By knowing that piece and information and knowing his husband's reactions, Lorne can manipulate Greg and get what he wants.

It's these small interactions that manipulators need most so pay close attention to how many questions they ask about your life. And pay attention to how much they share with you after they get the answers they want.

A manipulator would be hyper curious about your life or your friends or family. The victim would voluntarily share this with a boyfriend/girlfriend/partner maybe even a close friend. If the manipulator seems to provide nothing to contribute to the stream of information they get, be careful with what is shared.

For example, Tammy knows everything about Veronika's life, but Veronika knows nothing about hers. Tammy would always ask her best friend to talk about her life, but Veronika would provide little to nothing in retort. It's important to pay close attention to that information as well.

It could be basic, easily relatable topics to avoid talking about their real life and intentions. Or they could even set up for manipulation in the future by planting false stories about their lives into the conversation.

Manipulators will make sure that the victim is dependent purely on them, constantly creating a situation where they would be the higher authority and not be able to lose the rank they have over the victim. Taking them out of their comfort zone would be the most important part.

They would never let them go to a place where the victim could be superior.

For example, Frank doesn't want to go with Amy to her favorite diner. Frank prefers his diner because he's the important one and they care more about him than they would his date. He also wants Amy to think he's better than what she believes he is. Frank talks up the diner and convinces Amy to go with him to the diner. Being in that diner, Amy hears stories about Frank's childhood and learns only about the parts of his life that Frank wants her to know. A manipulator will censor the content that is available to you and make it impossible for you to look past the manipulation.

Censoring what you know can also come in the form of overusing information. A manipulator will spend more time correcting you. They will question your intelligence and won't believe you if you claim to know any information. To the manipulator the victim is always wrong and doesn't know anything.

They will do whatever they can to make sure the only information the victim ever receives comes from them. Pay attention to how much they correct the small things you do; watch the number times this occurs and watch how they do it.

A manipulator might prevent them from going online or checking their phones or would get mad at them for trying to source check any information they come across during the relationship.

For example, Tom is with Jane. Tom doesn't want Jane to know anything about his past and gets angry with her every time she tries to look up anything. Tom deleted all photos on his social media accounts that had any inkling to him having any former partners as well as his old drug use. Tom doesn't want Jane to see anything before she started seeing him and when she asks about his past, Tom tells Jane he was a good student and didn't get into any trouble.

Chapter 6: History Of Persuasion

Persuasion has a long history, going back to when humans discovered how to use it to our advantage. Persuasion is defined as a type of behavior that is employed as a means to influence someone's way of thinking, beliefs, decisions, motivation, and behavior.

It can be subtle and undetectable, done covertly, or more obvious, such as a form of encouragement.

The reasons for persuasion vary and are commonly used for personal and/or financial gain. It's a method applied throughout history for political and social gain. One notable example is how the Greeks viewed forms of persuasion, as a way to measure the suitability of a politician or position of authority. The ability to persuade was valued highly, and those who were successful were regarded as worthy of election.

Aristotle, a Greek philosopher, regarded persuasion as an essential skill to acquire and develop for a variety of reasons. It can be argued that persuasion, if used in its most skillful form, can deflect many negative attributes and help someone gain favor, regardless of the circumstance. An example of this is a court case, where a defendant or their lawyer can argue their innocence by way of persuasion. Even where a defendant is believed to be guilty, persuasion can (and has), convince a judge or jury that evidence is circumstantial or that a witness's testimony is not credible.

There is more to this method than simply convincing an individual or group of a certain belief or concept with a smooth presentation and convincing words; it includes a far more in-depth study and observation of the people who are to be persuaded. Many of these attributes are useful in winning an argument or a case, whether the person employing the persuasion techniques is correct or not. In some cases, it's not about right or wrong, but instead, a variance in opinions or beliefs where persuasion can go a long way to convince people to see the other side of the debate.

What Are The Different Types Of Persuasion?

Rhetoric is a powerful method of persuasion, which involves the careful study and observation of people, either in groups, as individuals or in society, to better understand how best to apply the "art" of persuasion. Observing people would entail many studies, including employing skilled writers, artists, and speakers with the expertise and talent to persuade. A modern example of this method can be seen in advertisements aimed at specific demographics to promote the sale of a product, or a political campaign targeting undecided voters, to sway their decision one way or another.

The goal is not only to get your attention but also to maintain it by "speaking" to you in a way that evokes an emotional response or action. This could result in an emotional plea to support one political party instead of others or to purchase a certain product or service because of a certain nostalgia or connection with family or co-workers.

The reasons for using persuasive techniques is not always secretive or malicious: it can be a good way to convince someone to reconsider making the wrong decision that could result in a detrimental outcome, or serve as a form of positive encouragement or reinforcement as a form of empowerment, such as "you can do it" and "what have you got to lose, come on!" When persuasion takes on a more direct tone, it may seem like a strong form of encouragement. While this may work for some people, it doesn't have the same impact on others. Some people thrive on overt persuasion and may otherwise not achieve a milestone or "go for it" without that persuasive push. On the other hand, some people prefer more autonomy and do not respond well. This is where covert or more subtle forms of persuasion can be useful in influencing them.

Recognizing the different signs of persuasion is key to knowing if someone is using these methods on you. It may not be as obvious as coaxing someone to change their mind or try something new. Some forms of persuasion may be subtle and difficult to detect initially.

Understanding the reasons behind persuasive techniques and the different purposes they serve can help determine if you may be on the receiving end and the reasons why.

Three Basic Forms Of Persuasion

There are three types of persuasion: ethos, logos, and pathos, according to

Aristotle. Each method appeals to a different source and has its reason for use:

Ethos

Ethos is known as the persuasion using ethics or morality as a basis. In this method of persuasion, the speaker or individual applying this method is trustworthy, credible, and knowledgeable. In their speech or debate, a credible person will make use of their related expertise and knowledge to support their argument. This is done by citing relevant sources and using their credibility as an expert to persuade the listener of their legitimacy.

This method is regarded as respectful in that it doesn't intend to sway the listener for unethical gain or advantage.

The speaker's reputation and status carry a lot of weight in terms of credibility, though this can also be established by using carefully constructed arguments that show that they are ethical.

Logos

Logos is based primarily in logic, or the application of logic to reason with or persuade someone. This method involves using evidence and related studies to support an argument.

A clear, concise form doesn't convince someone based on pseudo-science or skewed facts, but rather, it appeals to people who are not easily persuaded unless facts and their related sources support the argument. The format of logos is usually presented in a clear, sometimes chronological and progressive manner to show how a subject or topic began as disputable, followed by studies and observation to gain factual information to support the argument.

Pathos

Pathos is a method of persuasion that uses the emotion of the recipient (the person being persuaded). This is one of the most powerful and frequently used methods of persuasion. Pathos appeals to an audience's emotions, including their passions, imagination, creativity, and sympathetic nature. While the aim of this method is similar to logos and ethos, pathos can become very deceptive is using a vulnerable person's or group's emotions to their advantage. This can be seen in high control groups, where the promise of making lots of money or reaping the rewards of following a set of rules or belief system. Emotional persuasion can also be powerful in helping the audience identify with the speaker and/or their supporters, by sharing personal experiences and anecdotes that can convince people they are sincere and genuine, or "just one of us." The danger with employing pathos is how it can be misused to take advantage of a vulnerable or gullible group of people who are looking for quick answers and solutions to their problems.

Chapter 7: How To Spot A Fellow Manipulator

While manipulating others might be gainful to you, being manipulated by someone else is definitely not. It is for this reason that it is just as important to know how to spot a manipulator as it is to know how to manipulate.

Some people are simply born manipulators blessed with the gift of the gab, and these natural-born manipulators all seem to share some common traits as described by psychiatrist, Abigail Brenner.

- They are incapable of true altruism. Manipulative people hardly, if ever, do something out of the goodness of their hearts—there is usually an ulterior motive. For example, a manipulative person might buy you lunch today, and while you'd think that they were simply being generous, the aforementioned manipulative person would actually be planning to ask you to work one of their shifts tomorrow.

• They're big talkers, but that is where it ends. Manipulators do not usually follow up their grandiose speeches or ideas with actual action. They build these incredible castles in the sky to draw you in, without the intention of ever acting on any of the commitments or promises they might make. For example, your boss may continually hint at a promotion before every big project they assign to you, but has no intention to actually promote you—they're simply trying to manipulate you into giving 110% to a project in the hope of furthering your career.

• They are not empathetic. Manipulators either choose not to empathize with others or are simply incapable of empathy. You might spot a manipulator in this way, for example, when your company is undergoing downsizing. Under normal circumstances, even the employees who are not being laid off will feel sad and sorry for their colleagues who are losing their jobs, but a manipulator may be smug, or perhaps entirely apathetic, about their colleagues' misfortune.

- They are better gossips than your average high school girl. Manipulators enjoy watching people squirm—and what better way to do this than by spreading malicious stories or by sharing the blunders of others with the world? Your colleague standing at the watercooler telling everyone about Sarah's divorce, and reveling in the gory details, might be revealing themselves to be a manipulator.

- They will misuse even the smallest kindness you might show them. If you give manipulators an inch, they take a mile. Manipulators take advantage of people, it is simply what they do—and there's no easier way for them to do this than if you have already opened the door to their abuse by doing them a favor or by being kind to them. An example of this might be if you brought your coworker coffee for the morning meeting one day, and suddenly, this is what is expected of you—and now this coworker gets upset when they arrive at the meeting and their cup of coffee is not already waiting for them. This coworker might be a manipulator.

- They like to play the blame game. Manipulators don't want to accept responsibility for their own wrongdoings, so they attempt to assign the blame to someone else—even if it means ruining that person's career, relationships, or friendships. An example of this might be that one coworker who made a blunder on a project they had been working on, but when confronted blamed the team leader for their failure or incompetence—resulting in their team leader losing their job. A manipulator would happily sacrifice somebody else's career in this way.

● They do not have boundaries. At all. Manipulators usually do not understand, or do not care about, the social contract prescribing the rules of etiquette to which the rest of us subscribe. A manipulator might ask you questions that are just a little too personal, or might call you about a work-related matter at an unreasonable hour, or might show up at your house unexpectedly. They don't understand, or don't care about, the concept of being "rude."

● They are unwilling to compromise. It's their way or the highway. Manipulators insist on things being done exactly as they expect them to be done. Whether this is due to a need to insist on having authority or whether this is an inborn defect is unknown. And when they do not get their way, the resulting outburst is often incredibly aggressive and explosive. For this reason, people are often wary of going against a manipulator, which is why so many of them allegedly end up in higher management positions.

Of course, the other "natural-born" manipulator that is important to be able to spot is the psychopath. According to Amy Morin, psychotherapist and author of 13 Things Mentally Strong People Do Not Do, psychopaths share five common traits.

They think that they are important. Very important. Psychopaths tend to have a grandiose sense of self, and often think of themselves as the center of the universe. As a result of this inflated ego, psychopaths often demand special, or superior, treatment. They expect to be treated as the royalty they believe themselves to be—and all hell breaks loose when their incredibly high standards are not met.

They are incapable of feeling guilt or remorse. Psychopaths do not have a conscience. They are able to contemplate things which would make others rile back in disgust, gagging at the very thought. Psychopaths are often born with an underdeveloped or maldeveloped frontal lobe, impacting their ability to feel empathy or understand what is morally right or morally wrong. As a result of this, they are often capable of acts of incredible cruelty.

They are master manipulators. Here, you can refer back to the common traits of manipulators listed above. Psychopaths are fantastically talented at guilt-tripping others, and equally gifted at flattery and seduction. You might find yourself unknowingly, or unwittingly, obeying a psychopath's every command due to their ability to manipulate.

They are incredibly charming. This slots into the flattery and seduction mentioned above. Psychopaths are very good at getting people to be "on their team." They smile and joke their way into the lives of the people around you, and these people are often unable to see the psychopath for what they truly are. A psychopath will have the entire neighbourhood wrapped around their finger in notime. They might even get elected for office.

They are also incredibly ruthless. You will absolutely know if you have crossed a psychopath in some way as they are likely to reciprocate through small (or large) acts of revenge. They are also more than happy to turn those who are nearest and dearest to you against you, if they feel that you have wronged them in some way. A psychopath usually dispenses his or her own justice, usually with disastrous effects.

But how can you pick a psychopath out of the crowd? Prakash Masand, founder of the Centers of Psychiatric Excellence, believes there are eight signs that suggest someone is a psychopath.

- They are irresponsible and have no regard for the safety of others. A prime example of this is the Wall Street bankers who toppled the United States into an economic crisis in 2008 due to underhanded hedge fund trading with derivatives. Many of them were aware that they would be driving others to bankruptcy, but still went ahead and did it for their own personal gain.

- They violate the rights of others. An example of this would be the case of Robert Maxwell, the incredibly wealthy publishing giant, who, after his death, was found to have stolen millions by defrauding the pension funds of thousands of innocent people.

- They engage in socially irresponsible behavior like binge drinking, addiction to narcotics, promiscuous sexual activity, or other criminal activities. An example of a psychopath engaging in socially irresponsible (or rather, reprehensible) behavior is Ted Bundy, the infamous serial killer and promising law student who confessed to murdering 30 women in his spare time.

- They are frequently in trouble with the law. This happens as a natural consequence of socially irresponsible behavior and violating the rights of others. Psychopaths are not always caught red-handed for murder, though—sometimes, these transgressions are as small as not believing that the speed limit applies to them, thus amassing a small mountain of fines.

- They like to hurt others and are often sadists. An example of this is Ilse Koch, the wife of a Nazi secret service member, who would walk around naked in a Jewish concentration camp and had any man who so much as dared to glance at her shot on the spot.

● An inability to, or apathy toward, understanding right from wrong. Psychopaths either do not care about doing the right thing, or do not know that they are doing the wrong thing. An example of this is the "angel of mercy" stereotype found within the study of criminology. Offenders who fall under this stereotype commit murders with the belief that they are doing the victim a favor by euthanizing them.

● The tendency to lie. Often. Very often. Because psychopaths have no moral compass, they have no reason to be truthful if the truth is not gainful to them in one way or another. They have no problem with making up stories about themselves, either, whether they do it for sympathy or adoration.

Interestingly, Masand also found that men were more prone to psychopathy than women. Furthermore, psychopaths are more inclined to taking up certain professions. Kevin Dutton, the author of The Wisdom of Psychopaths: What Saints, Spies, and Serial Killers Can Teach Us About Success, formulated a list of ten professions which psychopaths are the most likely to pursue. According to Dutton's research, the highest ratio of psychopaths can be found among government officials/civil servants/politicians, chefs, clergymen (or clergywomen), police officers or military personnel, journalists, surgeons, salespeople, media personalities, lawyers, and chief executive officers (CEOs).

Scientists have actually formulated a physical test by means of which psychopaths can be identified. Studies have found that psychopaths' pupils do not dilate when they are shown gruesome or distressing images, while the average person's do. Thus, if you suspect someone of being a psychopath, you could theoretically show them a photo of a horrific accident scene, for example, and watch to see whether their pupils dilate.

On the other hand, it is also important to learn to spot people who will be easy to manipulate. According to Kim Saeed, the writer of 10 Essential Survivor Secrets to Liberate Yourself from Narcissistic Abuse, there are seven personality traits which those who are easy to manipulate all have in common.

The need to fix and heal those around them. Those who are easy to manipulate are always on the lookout for someone down on their luck to help out of the gutter. The reason this makes them easy to manipulate is that absolutely anybody can pretend to be going through a hard time, and in doing so win the loyalty and trust of the aforementioned person.

An inability to set boundaries or to say "no." Those who are easy to manipulate are generally so scared of confrontation that they are not willing to spark an argument by being resistant or by voicing their opinion. This specific trait is easy to exploit for obvious reasons—if they just can not say no, you can burden them with favors and expectations, and anticipate no resistance in return.

Honesty and compassion. Being honest makes you particularly manipulatable because your greatest weaknesses and loftiest aspirations are all absolutely apparent to those around you. Compassion, on the other hand, is the driving force for the first point of this list. Being overly compassionate opens you up to manipulation by those who are willing to play the victim, as master manipulators always are.

Stubbornness. Those who are easy to manipulate generally refuse to give up on their mission to save the very person who is manipulating them. This stubbornness leads them to tolerate behavior which they would not have tolerated under normal circumstances, thus making them easy targets for manipulation.

Unconditional love. Those who are the absolute easiest to manipulate are those who unconditionally love the manipulator (parents, siblings, romantic partners, friends, etc.). The reason for this is that, regardless of the kind of treatment that they are forced to endure, they continue to love the manipulator. This love is an exploitable weakness.

Being trusting. People who are easy to manipulate believe anything you tell them, this is also known as "being too trusting." Some people are simply naïve, while others perhaps only see the best in the manipulator and refuse to acknowledge the uglier side—regardless of the reason, some people are easier to deceive than others.

Being too polite or respectful. Manipulators actively seek out those who will not call them out in public, and who better to target than those who are too coy to say something when they are made to feel uncomfortable? Being overly polite also makes one more likely to agree to small favors which, as discussed earlier, makes one more likely to agree to larger and larger favors as time passes.

Similarly, it is just as important to know some tactics to avoid being manipulated yourself. The author of Are You Too Nice? How to Gain Appreciation and Respect, Ni Preston, developed eight techniques to avoid being manipulated.

The first technique he described is by far the easiest to abide by. It simply involves practicing the art of saying "no." If you feel uncomfortable with what is being asked of you, firmly say no. You do not necessarily need to be confrontational in doing this—

a simple, "Sorry, I do not have time," will likely suffice.

The second technique is to set consequences. You need to handle a manipulator a little bit like you might handle a child: he or she needs to know the rules, and when he or she breaks these rules, there needs to be a "punishment." An example of how you could use this is by telling a person, "I am uncomfortable talking with you about that. If you continue to talk about it, I will report you to human resources." Manipulators do not want to get in trouble, so when trying to avoid being manipulated, make sure that you follow through on the rules and corresponding consequences which you have set.

The third technique is remembering that your time is your own, and you are allowed to take it. Manipulators will usually demand an answer to their requests immediately, in the hope of pressuring you into complying. You can circumnavigate this manipulative technique simply by saying, "I'll think about it." You don't have to follow a manipulator's timeline, and you are certainly not obligated to answer anything straight away.

The fourth technique involves asking manipulators probing questions when they make requests of you. Next time a manipulator asks you to do something for them, consider responding with, "Are you asking me, or telling me?" or "What do I get out of this?" or "Are you really expecting me to do that?" Chances are, you will catch the manipulator off-guard and perhaps even get them to withdraw the request completely (at the very least, it will force them to pause for a second and consider whether what they are doing is right).

The fifth technique is to avoid letting the manipulator make you feel guilty. You are not obligated to do anyone any favors, and thus you have nothing to feel guilty about. Manipulators make their targets feel guilty in the hope that they will eventually feel so bad about themselves that they will give in to the manipulator's will.

The sixth technique is to keep your distance. If you know that somebody is manipulating you (or trying to), do not give them any opportunities to do so by spending time with them. It is honestly good advice just to give a manipulator a wide berth and to avoid getting pulled into their games altogether.

The seventh technique is to know your rights. Manipulators will go out of their way to violate them. Remind yourself regularly that you have the right to be treated with respect, to set your own priorities, to have a differing opinion, and to express your feelings.

The eighth, and final, technique is to confront the manipulator. Publicly. A manipulator will generally avoid the public eye, and by calling them out, you are likely to put them off trying to manipulate you ever again.

Chapter 8: Mind Control

Wouldn't it be easier if you could close your eyes and control your thoughts? Yeah, unfortunately, impossible. Or maybe? A brief introduction to mind control enables mind control. No, customers, partners, and step-parents cannot be turned into meaningless zombies, but they can. Sure, there is science. In the 1980s, a researcher named Robert Chardini named Dr. Influence: The Persuasive Psychology. He outlined various principles and methods that have been scientifically proven to affect people. Since then, this is the most important book in the marketing industry.

The bad news is:

Mind control is not a magical power, esoterics, or shaking and rolling a wheelchair (although I was tempted). The truth is that it hurt many people:

The truth about marketing

The marketing hub is not a customer specification or market segment or complex nonsense taught by most business schools. It is endlessly simple and can be combined into one word: yes.

When he asks a blogger for a link, he says, "yes." Have the partner promote the product, and they say "yes." When he asks the customer for a certificate, he says, "yes." If you get enough, your business/blog/charity will win. Otherwise, this will fail. It's easy, but few people know how to do it.

The good news is that you can learn.

Here's a guide for marketers to control their minds. Use these seven strategies wisely.

1. Think everything for them

The worst mistake you can make when asking someone is saying, "Remember it." That's why people have a lot to think about. Between her work, her family, and her own hobbies and friends, her ideas are already packed like suitcases that stretch along the edge. Adding another sock will explode the whole. To avoid this, they "forget" what is most important to them, or they don't think much when they think about you. It's not because you're lazy or stupid. You are busy, and you are not at the top of the priority list. So the best strategy is not to get them to think.

Instead of expecting a blog post to benefit your audience, explain it, and give examples of similar posts that have improved in the past. Instead of asking to host a webinar, set up a webinar, landing page, and email yourself and send it as part of the pitch. Instead of asking the customer to create a new certificate, send various examples to use as a guide. Accurately. Please explain your reasoning.

Proof. Tell them what to do next and why. If you do it right, it doesn't look like you're listening. This is educational. I will say yes. It was a child's play because it was thinking about everything, not for the magical power of impulses.

2. Start the avalanche

Building a successful marketing campaign is like starting an avalanche. After climbing the mountain first, there is a huge rock on it, and then it is difficult to sweat and mumble and push the rock. Of mountain waterfall. Lesson? The first big yes is ass pain, but if you get it from the right person, it's easy to get the next one.

For example:

Popular bloggers can tweet your posts, but when you do, dozens or even hundreds of people retweet them. It can be difficult to convince a niche leader to advertise a product, but once it is successful, everyone else will want to promote it. It's hard to trust a key customer, but once you do, it's easy to increase sales and get more credentials. Of course, many marketers recommend the opposite approach. They tell you to start from the bottom up and make your way easier, so work your way up.

In fact, it is an illusion. Yes, it is easier to squeeze smaller stones than squeeze rocks, but stones are more likely to cause avalanches. It takes a lot of effort to get the best people to help you at first, but in the long run, there will be less work, and the results will be huge.

3. Wait a minute and earn miles

Did you hear the phrase, "Wait a minute, take a mile"? It should be easy. This is said to be a mitigation warning. It should protect you from using it. But this is great marketing. When you ask for something, don't listen to everything first. Instead, start small. It's easy to get started. Reduce the risk of failure. Let's see the results for yourself. If this works, please give me more. Further. Further. You may think this is unfair, but if all goes well, why not push too much? This is not an operation. This is common sense

For example:

When creating a guest post for a popular blog, first suggest your idea in a paragraph or two, submit an outline, and then create an entire post. You are a JV with a field leader. If you want to advertise, send her initial content to 10% of the list, over 50% of the list, and then 100%. Then run a direct mail campaign.

If you want to give your clients a case study, request 1-3 sentences, request a half-page statement and then talk about your success in a two-hour webinar. It's not a psychological trick or anything. It's smart business. No one wants to risk everything in advance. By offering engagement gradually, you have the opportunity to say yes to them.

4. Always keep a proper deadline

The keyword is "real." We all said to the salesman, "Now that afternoon we have three more options, so it's good to come back soon. I don't know how long this will take." No customers, no hurry. Not only does the salesman sacrifice your trust, but he also sacrifices his sales, and he is happy to lie. And it's not just a seller. How many times have you set a complete artificial deadline because you think others will inspire you to act? Our teacher did it, our boss did it, our family didn't, and you probably did, without even thinking about it.

Not only is it useless, but it also doesn't matter. It is easy to create real urgency. With a little thought, it can be integrated with marketing. For example: Instead of always leaving a free report on your blog, let everyone know that it's only seven days before you charge. Not only do you get more downloads, but other bloggers often promote them on Windows

· Others can help you decide when to advertise your products. Instead of authorizing a partner, plan a launch, announce on a list, and send notifications to invite partners. Instead of requesting credentials when a customer arrives, indicate a future release schedule, including a specific date for submitting credentials. Until then, you will not need it or be able to integrate it. Will some of them say goodbye and say they are too busy now to catch up next time? Indeed, it's better than not starting everything. What happens when you allow others to decide on a schedule.

5. Give ten times more than you take

Do you know what you have to give before getting it? But what you don't know is how much to give. Many vendors misunderstand the 1:1 ratio. Before requesting a link, you must provide the link. Before you can request a promotion, you must run the promotion. Before seeking testimony, you must do something worthy of testimony. But it was wrong. Smart marketers use a 10:1 ratio. This is not only active but also:

If you need 100 visitors, send 1,000

If you sell a product for $ 1,000, sell the product for $ 10,000 first

If you need a certificate, run ten different customer service initiatives covered by the certificate

This is "You hurt my back, and I hurt your back" It's all about generosity, and you can't say no.

Yes, this is a daunting task, but a price for influence.

6. Confront something bigger than yourself

Imagine two homeless people on a street corner. The first man has the usual sign, "Save a few dollars. Bless God." On the other hand, the second boy says, "I can't eat my family." What do I need to help? Second, isn't it? Forget to give him a few dollars. With such a mark, you can take him to a grocery store and buy $ 200 groceries, I know to do that, it represents something bigger than yourself Power and caring for people, this applies to everything:

Instead of writing another guide, comment on important topics and discuss with curiosity and unexplained logic

Instead of setting up another consulting company, make constant efforts to change the lives of clients

Sell a philosophy full of heroic examples to motivate customers instead of selling another step-by-step guide

These are the things people want to talk about. They are grateful that they can help spread the word to you.

7. Completely shy

Want to know what distinguishes a big seller from a mediocre seller? I have not mentioned a lack of conscience, a sociable and straightforward personality, or any other way our marketers have traditionally seen. These stereotypes are often myths. No, shamelessly, I mean:

What you are doing is good for the world and an unwavering conviction that you will be willing to do anything to make it happen. If you trust your content, don't forget to publish it. Advertise daily, weekly, monthly, and annually, pass the message on to everyone who needs to hear it, and refuses to rest until they retire.

Don't balk sell if you trust your product. You enjoy it. Not because you are greedy, pessimistic, or selfish, but because you know that your product helps them, it is your duty to buy them. Take your life

Don't ask for donations if you believe in philanthropy. You challenge them. Hold people by your shoulders and look at them and tell them what you are doing will change the world, and then they will play their part.

This is not about money. Not even the legacy. Love. It is fascinating. It is a must for the most beautiful and you have to fight to do it. Do you have such a vision? Is there something to fight for every day? In this way, everything can be reached nearby. If you What are the points?

Chapter 9: The Trojan In Your Head

We all have the ability to be our own worst enemies. People with bad intentions will use this against us if we allow them to.

Using mind games to mentally manipulate a person is an insidious act that tears at a person's sanity.

Anything that so deeply hurts and scars a person isn't nice to do and we all know that. Yet, we all have done some of these things and some of these things have been done to us.

Knowing what these things can do to a person will help you to know when you must use these mind tricks and when they are being used on you.

Once you can recognize these tricks as they are taking place, you won't become a victim of mind games anymore.

Disqualifying

This act is really hurtful. You not only deliberately want to hurt someone's feelings, but you are also going to give them a double-shot of your viper tongue.

For example – Sheila doesn't like the fact that her friend, Ashley is prettier than her. So, she often uses a tactic to throw Ashely off about her appearance.

"You did not dye your hair again, Ashley? What a mistake," Sheila says very loudly, to purposely draw the attention of their classmates.

With wide eyes, Ashely runs her hand through her golden blonde hair. "What?"

Before everyone around them sees Sheila as a real meanie, she says, "I didn't mean to hurt your feelings, Ash – it's just that your hair looks like a haystack."

Double whammy!

Forgetting

This age-old tactic for messing with someone's mind can be so mean that it defies reason.

Here's an example-

Jane came home from work with a splitting headache only to find that the aspirin bottle is empty. "Oh, Charlie took the last one and didn't bother to toss the empty bottle out so I would know that we had none left! I'll call him and ask him to please bring more home."

She did let her husband know about the aspirin then went to take a hot bath to see if that would help with the pain until he got home with the medicine.

But when he comes home with empty hands, she asks, "Where is the medicine, honey?"

"Oh, I forgot about that completely. I'm sorry."

"It was only a half-hour ago. How could you forget?"

"I got a call and drove past all the stores. Sorry."

He's not the one with a splitting headache and it's glaringly apparent that his wife doesn't rank very high on his caring meter.

Persecuting

Have you ever been the one who does everything wrong?

Or have you been the one pointing out how someone else always does everything wrong?

Using persecution to make a person feel like less of a person is the way to go here. Telling them that they always let you down, lets them feel bad about themselves.

And if someone is telling you that you always do something that bothers them, then it's you who are at the wrong end of this deal.

Whichever end you are on, you can stop it from continuing. Simply state that no one is always or never anything. We all do things in varying degrees. So, don't be this person and if you are the one being persecuted, then don't stand for it.

Guilt Tripping

My mother lived to take us all on guilt trips. No matter how much easier it would've been to get us to do something, she had to go the extra mile to make us feel horrible over something first.

An actual guilt-tripping story here folks-

"Can you go out and bring in the Sunday paper?" she asked me.

I was a helpful kid. "Sure, Mom."

Just as I got to the paper that lay on the stone path in front of our home, the sprinkler came on and shot me right in the face. I grabbed the newspaper anyway and fled the scene. And just as I was shaking the water off my body, I saw my mother standing by the faucet. She'd turned it on, on purpose.

As if she hadn't noticed a thing, she held out her hand to receive the paper. I wasn't sure if she'd meant to soak me or not. Feeling confused, I walked up to her and just as before I got to her, I tripped over one of the stones that had been moved out of place.

I fell right into her, knowing her down on her bottom. "Why'd you do that?" she screamed at me.

"I tripped. I didn't do it on purpose." I scrambled up and reached out to take her hand to help her up.

"Don't touch me!" she snapped at me. "I can do it myself."

"Sorry," I said, and I meant it. I hadn't meant to knock her down at all.

"You got me all wet too. Yuck." She got up on her own with only a slightly damp spot on her shirt.

I was drenched. "Um." I gestured to my wet state.

Shaking her head as if she didn't even notice my current state, she snatched the paper from me then turned away from me. "Just give it to me. I asked a simple thing from you. I didn't realize it would cost me so much. Now my back hurts and my shirt is ruined. Thanks a lot."

Demoralized, I could only stand there, feeling guilty about what? I wasn't sure.

But there was lots of guilt and believe it or not, she got to keep me on that guilt trip for a solid week. I would be at her beck and call, doing everything she asked of me. And she asked a lot!

Gaslighting

This mind trick is so dark that I hate even to let people know it exists. But I only do it so that you can see it when and if it happens to you.

Not everyone is handed this particular mind trick mostly because you have to be at least half-evil to play it.

So it goes like this – you know that what someone is saying really happened. But you want them to think they're losing their minds. And by the time you are finished with them, they just might.

Example –

"You know that coffee shop we used to go to all the time, Brad?" June asked her long-time boyfriend.

"You mean the ice cream shop, June. I don't even drink coffee," he said.

"No, it was a coffee shop. And you stopped drinking coffee a few years ago. But you and I did drink coffee when we first started dating." She recalls it perfectly.

"Not me, I guess," he states.

"It was you," she insists. "There was green trim around the tables. You remember. And that's where we found we loved caramel in our coffee."

Shaking his head, he's adamant. "I have never liked coffee, June. And I wouldn't even go into a coffee shop. It. Wasn't. Me."

"It was you!" She knows it was him. She doesn't recall ever going to that coffee shop with anyone else. And it's not the first time he's pulled this on her either.

If you find someone doing this to you, remove yourself from their company. They are the worst kind of manipulators who only seek to destroy everything about you.

Shaming

People who shame others express themselves by trying to point out people who say or do something they want others to believe isn't morally right. It's when a person is so quick to point out things about others to everyone who will listen, so they don't look at them too hard.

I'm sure you've heard the expression when you're pointing at someone else, only one finger is aimed at them while you have three of your own fingers pointing back at you. This stems from people who love making others the center of ridicule, thusly taking the attention of others away from them.

As if they were even paying attention to them in the first place.

The worst part is that these people most often form jealousy about someone, then try to dig up anything on them to make them look bad. This is also known as piling up dead bodies to walk upon to make yourself look taller.

It's just bad mojo, karma, or whatever your particular idea of paying for the bad things you do is. I wouldn't use this at all, nor for any reason. If you truly have beef with someone, hash it out with them, without trying to defame them.

Pretending

Why do people pretend about anything, you ask?

Well, to avoid dealing with honest emotions and conflict of course.

You could be out at a club and someone from the opposite sex might come up to you with some words that flatter you and you might actually believe that they're into you in a big way.

But here's the thing about situations like that and lots of others where people are able to make sexual advances without it seeming gross and unwanted. You have gone to a bar, a nightclub, a social situation of any kind really. This means you are out, and you might be looking for some action.

There are many people who simply want some sexual action and are willing to lie about their true interests just to get what they want. After the deed is done, they will disappear and refuse to take your calls and texts. They never wanted you for more than one thing.

Does this hurt?

Well, of course, it does. But the thing to know is that you shouldn't do an instant hookup anyway if you're vulnerable to being flattered and falling into bed with people who never meant a thing they said.

And never think that only the male gender of our human species does this, the females do this just as much as the males do.

What about when someone is mad, and they pretend not to be. Now, this one is done most often by females, but males can do it too. And the way this plays out is never nice either.

If a woman is mad and she says she's not, her man better walks on eggshells for the next week or even longer, and he better watch out for everything. She could merely wash his whites with reds to turn them pink, to cutting the brake lines on his car. It's that bad.

Ghosting

Disappearing, not answering calls, or texts is sometimes seen as someone trying to avoid you or let you know that they're mad at you. And there are times that is true.

The main reason people ghost others is to see if others actually care about them.

Janice, "He's called eighteen times in the last three hours. Yeah, it's safe to say he does like me. But I'm still gonna leave him waiting the whole day to make sure he's into me."

If you find someone doing that to you, don't waste your time on them. They have a host of things you will have to go through before they ever admit their feelings for you if they're capable of forming real feelings in the first place.

The thing to know about people who do things like this, right from the very beginning, is they could have a personality disorder that might make living life with them in it extremely difficult.

Key Takeaways

If someone tells you that they forgot something important you asked them to do, you should see this as a mind game.

If you begin to feel as if someone is persecuting you, this is a mind game.

Using guilt to get someone to do what you want them to is playing with a person's mind.

Gaslighting is an insidious act that actually scrapes at a person's sanity, making them think that things happened that didn't or that things didn't happen then did.

When someone tries to make you feel ashamed of something, they are using your mind against you.

Pretending that you don't hear someone or see someone is just another mind game.

Ghosting is used to get someone to miss you. Be above that.

Exercises

You're looking hot out at the club. But you're not looking for anything more than someone to dance with. So when Jane — the sexy babe asks you to dance, then starts telling you how she saw you across the room and couldn't take her eyes off you, do you jump right in and get on board with her taking you home?

A new man in your life has just told you that something you knew happened, didn't happen. What do you do next?

Your spouse has thrown out half your closet of clothes because they deemed them inappropriate and unflattering, what do you do?

Are playing mind games ever an okay thing to do to other people? And why or why not?

Chapter 10: Developing Mind Control

Mind control involves using influence and persuasion to change the behaviors and beliefs in someone. That someone might be the person they or it might be someone else. Mind control has also been referred to as brainwashing, thought reform, coercive persuasion, mental control, and manipulation, just to name a few. Some people feel that everything is done by manipulation. But if that is true to are believed, then important points about manipulation will be lost. Influence is much better thought of as a mental continuum with two extremes. One side has influences that are respectful and ethical and work to improve the individual while showing respect for them and their basic human rights. The other side contains influences that are dark and destructive that work to remove basic human rights from a person, such as independence, the ability for rational thought, and sometimes their total identity.

When thinking of mind control, it is better to see it as a way to use influence on other people that will disrupt something in them, like their way of thinking or living. Influence works on the very basis of what makes people human, such as their behaviors, beliefs, and values. It can disrupt the very way they chose personal preferences or make critical decisions. Mind control is nothing more than using words and ideas to convince someone to say or do something they might never have thought of saying or doing on their own.

There are scientifically proven methods that can be used to influence other people. Mind control has nothing to do with fakery, ancient arts, or even magical powers. Real mind control really is the basis of a word that many people hate to hear. That word is marketing. Many people hate to hear that word because of the negative connotations associated with it. When people hear "marketing," they automatically assume that it refers to those ideas taught in business school. But the basis of marketing is not about deciding which part of the market to target or deciding which customers will likely buy this product. The basis of marketing is one very simple word. That word is "YES."

If a salesperson asks a regular customer to write a brief endorsement of the product they buy, hopefully, they will say yes. If someone asks their significant other to take some of the business cards to pass out at work, hopefully, they will say yes. If you write any kind of blog and ask another blogger to provide a link to yours on their blog, hopefully, they will say yes. When enough people say yes, the business or blog will begin to grow. With even more yesses, it will continue to grow and thrive.

This is the very simple basis of marketing. Marketing is nothing more than using mind control to get other people to buy something or to do something beneficial for someone else. And the techniques can easily be learned.

The first technique in mind control is to tell people what you want them to want. Never tell people to think it over or take some time. That is a definite mind control killer. When they are told to think something over they will not. It will be forgotten, and then it will never happen. This has nothing to do with being stupid or lazy and everything to do with just being way too busy.

So the best strategy is to take the offensive and think for them. Everything must be explained in the beginning. Never assume that the other blogger will automatically understand the benefits of adding a link will be for them. Do not expect anyone to give a demonstration blindly. And merely asking for a testimonial, while it might garner an appositive response, probably will not garner a well-formed testimonial to the product. Instead, be prepared to explain the blog, show examples, and offer compelling reasons why this merger will be a benefit to both parties. Have the demonstration laid out in great detail with notes on what to say when and visuals to go along with the notes, so all the other person has to do is present the information. Offer the customer a few variations of testimonials that have already been received and ask them to choose one and personalize it a bit. Always be specific in explaining what is desired. Explain why it is desired. Show how this will work. Tell the person how to do it and why they should do it. If done correctly it will feel exactly like one friend advising another friend on which is the best path to take. And the answer will be yes simply because saying yes makes so much sense.

Think of the avalanche. Think of climbing all the way to the top of the highest mountain ever. Now, at the top, think of searching for the biggest heaviest boulder that exists on the mountain. Now, picture summoning up superhuman strength to push this boulder, dislodging it from the place it has rested for years and years. Once this boulder is loosened, it rolls easily over the edge of the cliff, crashing into thousands of other boulders on its way down the mountain, taking half of the mountain with it in a beautiful cascade of rocks and dirt. Imagine sitting there smiling cheerfully at the avalanche that was just created.

Marketing and mind control are very like creating an avalanche. Getting the first person to answer yes might be difficult. But each subsequent yes will be easier and easier. And always start at the top, never the bottom. Starting at the top is definitely more difficult, and it is more likely to come with more negative responses than positive responses in the beginning. But starting at the top also yields a much greater reward when the avalanche does begin. And the results will be far greater than beginning at the bottom of the mountain. Yes, the small rock is easier to push over. Then it can be built upon by pushing over another small rock, then another. This way can work, but it will take much longer than being successful at the top. No one ever went fishing for the smallest fish in the pond or auditioned for the secondary role just to be safe. Everyone wants that top prize. Do not be afraid to go for it.

On the other hand, never ask for the whole boulder the first time. Ask for part of it. This may seem directly contradictory but it is not. Always start with a small piece. Make the beginning easier for everyone to see. Let other people use their own insight to see the end result. When the first bit goes well, then gradually ask for more and more and more.

Think of writing a guest spot for someone else who has their own blog. By sending in the entire manuscript first, there is a greater risk of rejection. Begin small. Send them a paragraph or two discussing them the idea. Then make an outline of the idea and send that in an email. Then write the complete draft you would like them too use and send it along. When asking a customer for a testimonial, start by asking for a few lines in an email. Then ask the customer to expand those few lines into a testimonial that covers at least half a typed page. Soon the customer will be ready for an hour-long webcast extolling the virtues of the product and your great customer service skills.

Everything must have a deadline that really exists. The important word here is the word 'real'. Everyone has heard the salesperson who said to decide quickly because the deal might not be available later or another customer was coming in and they might get it. That is a total fabrication and everyone knows it to be true. There is no impending other customers and the deal is not going to disappear. There is no real sense of urgency involved. But everyone does it. There are too many situations where people are given a totally fake deadline by someone who thinks it will instill a great sense of urgency for completion of the task. It is not only totally not effective but completely unneeded. It is a simple matter to create true urgency. Only leave free things available for a finite amount of time. When asking customers for testimonials is certain to mention the last possible day for it to be received to be able to be used. Some people will be unable to assist, but having people unable to participate is better than never being able to begin.

Always give before you receive. And do not ever think that giving is fifty-fifty. Always give much more than is expected in return. Before asking for a testimonial from a satisfied customer, be sure to make numerous acts of exceptional customer service. Before asking a blog writer for a link, link theirs to yours many times. This is not about helping someone out so they will help you. This is all about being so totally generous that the person who is asked for the favor cannot possibly say no. It might mean extra work, but that is how to influence other people.

Always stand up for something that is much bigger than average. Do not just write another blog on how to do something. Use an important issue to take a stand and defend the stance with unbeatable logic and fervent passion. Do not just write a how-to manual. Choose a particular idea and sell people on it, using examples of other people with the same idea living the philosophy.

Never feel shame. This does not mean being extremely extroverted to the point of silliness or having a total lack of conscience in business dealings. In the case of mind control shamelessness refers to a total complete belief that this course of action is the best possible course and everyone will benefit greatly from it. This is about writing the best possible blog ever and believing that everyone needs to read it to be able to improve their lives. It is about believing in a particular product so deeply that the feeling is that everyone will benefit from using it. It knows deep inside that this belief is the most correct belief ever and everyone should believe it.

Mind control uses the idea that someone's decisions and emotions can be controlled using psychological means. It is using powers of negotiation or mental influence to ensure the outcome of the interaction is more favorable to one person over the other. This is basically what marketing is: convincing someone to do something particular or buy something in particular. Being able to control someone else's mind merely means understanding the power of human emotion and being able to play upon those emotions. It is easier to have a mental impact on people if there is a basic understanding of human emotions. Angry people will back down when the subject of their anger is not afraid. Angry people feed upon the fear of others. Guilt is another great motivator. Making someone feels guilty for not thinking or feeling, in the same manner, is a wonderful way to get them to give in. Another way to use mind control over someone is to point out how valuable they are to the situation.

Mind control techniques

Some techniques were mentioned in the previous chapter. However, that was just to get you, the reader, acquainted with persuasion. Now, we are going to look a bit deeper into just how this is carried out. However, keep in mind what we discussed in the last chapter. We do not actually control someone else's mind. We guide them into doing that. It's important to remember this. The reason being that we need to always remember that the other person needs to see benefits and it helps for them to think that they are in control. This is a perfect quote to remember when trying to learn how to persuade someone else.

Some synonymous terms of mind control are brainwashing, thought reform, manipulation, exploitive persuasion, sociopsychological manipulation, behavioral change technology, and a few others.

There are a few different types of manipulation. Here, we are going to discuss 2 of those types. First, there is the sociopsychological manipulator. This is someone who attempts to use social influence in order to lead someone into a change in behavior or a decision. This can be indirect and deceptive in nature. It's also possible for this to be direct. With this form of manipulation, there is often great pressure put on the target individuals. An example of this is peer-pressure, but there are much bigger examples that we rarely notice.

We don't think of marketing as being this and it isn't usually negative in nature. One exception to this is with negative political ads. However, marketing is simply persuasion on a large scale. Let's look at television commercials. What are they exactly? Years ago, there were ads for cigarettes. Most of those who have a few years under the belt will probably remember the Marlboro Man. He was a healthy cowboy who portrayed a tough image. He was usually on horseback and sucking down a cigarette. We never saw anyone with cancer or being unable to breathe on those commercials. There were also numerous tobacco ads with very physically attractive people, both ladies and men, who were holding lit cigarettes in the ad. In reality, those who smoked for a long time usually looked anything but like the people portrayed on television and in the printed ads.

What about the commercials that attempt to lead us to believe that if we buy a certain product, our lives will somehow instantly become great? "Buy this drink and you will forever be ecstatic!" I like the pharmaceutical ads. "Are you feeling sad and depressed? Talk to your doctor about blah blah medication and kiss the sadness goodbye." There is no mention of what the possibilities for the cause of this sadness may be and how the best treatment is to stop what may be causing the problem, if possible, and not simply medicating it. They may even use pictures of cute little puppies or laughing children. They have associated something joyful and peaceful with their product leading you to subconsciously form the same connection. This is manipulation at its best. How about fast-food ads? It's a well-known fact that most people need to eat healthy in order to be physically fit. Eating this which are proven bad for you may not be a terrible thing if done in moderation but only in moderation. Have you ever seen an out-of-shape person on a fast-food ad?

When we are teenagers, in high-school, we are bombarded by psychological manipulation from all angles. We had to deal with the advertising seen on television and in magazines. We had to deal with growing up and listening to our parents. Then there was the, ever so dreaded, bombardment of peer-pressure. I am sure that everyone remembers this. Peer-pressure is simply the culmination of several kinds of social manipulation. This happens when outside ideas are placed in one person's head and then that individual passes them on. One child is made to believe that a brand of clothing is the best thing since sliced bread. Then he or she tells others that leading them to believe the same and to run to the store to buy them. This goes on and on. As time goes on, and we progress in technology, the pressure, and the manipulating, of teens is increasing at an exponential rate. Now, not only are kids pressured at school but due to social media, this is a never-ending cycle. It's worth mentioning that this all takes place without commonly being noticed and recognized for what it truly is. We call it "life" or "growing up" but what it is it really? It's mass manipulation.

Previously mentioned in this book, there is the beautiful art of political persuasion. We are constantly subjected to political ads and campaigns. Most of the time, important issues are thrown out of the window and candidate's pasts or mistakes, or transgressions, are brought to the forefront. A particular person may actually have the answers needed for positive change, but that does not matter when the political ads come out. We are led to forget that a certain candidate has an impeccable record of public service and good deeds and led to only think about one night that individual had too much to drink while back in college 20 years ago. This is becoming ever more prominent. Candidates don't even need to do this kind of advertising or manipulating, themselves. Anyone who can afford it can take it upon themselves and begin a smear campaign against someone and because of the way our brains work, if we see an ad enough times, we will begin to believe what we are being told.

Here, let us look at what we have learned, and are learning, about manipulation from another perspective. Let's look at it in a way that we can protect ourselves from it. Yes, you may be reading this book in order to learn how to do it, but you can also learn how to recognize that it's being done to you and how to block it. It begins with knowledge and mindfulness. If you are aware of these tactics and why they are being done, you are able to protect yourself from them. If you see a cute puppy on a tire commercial, know that puppies have nothing to do with car tires and that the commercial is only trying to manipulate your thinking and attempting to lead you into associating the two.

The examples for psychological manipulation are so numerous there could be an entire series of books written on this topic alone. However, for our purposes, we will move on to the other form of manipulation. Now, we are going to discuss a much darker method utilized to manipulate others. With this particular tactic, there is usually never a positive outcome for the target. This tactic is harmful to others and is not recommended for you to try in this book. Personally, I would rather you stay far away from this form of manipulation.

Now let's look at an emotional manipulator. Unlike with psychological manipulation, emotional manipulation is almost always negative and does harm to others. With this technique, the manipulator preys on the emotions of those in which he or she is targeting. Whatever the cause of this guilt, the manipulator will use it to his or her advantage. For instance, if a parent needed to cancel out on some outing with a child. Then the child brings that up at a later date as a reason for why that parent should or shouldn't do something. "Dad, you didn't take me to the record store last Friday. So, the least that you can do today is taking me to the clothing store." The child is playing on the fact that his or her father feels bad about not being able to take the child to the record store and is using that to persuade or manipulate him into going to buy some clothes.

One area where this manipulation often creeps up is with those suffering from addiction. This isn't simply referring to addicts. It includes their family, friends, and support network too. Actually, the ones who are not actually addicted are most likely to be the targets of emotional manipulation; Not the other way around. Why is this case?

Most addicts need to be rather intelligent and able to manipulate others. Otherwise, they probably wouldn't be able to be addicts. They wouldn't usually have the necessary resources. Addicts need those who are known as enablers. These are those who, with or without their knowledge, enable addicts to continue their use of whatever substance they desire. This can be with money or can be something like babysitting an addict's child so that the addict can go out and use. Most people wouldn't help with things like this, but they are put in positions where they see it best to go along with the program of helping that addict. One common method an addict will use here is emotional manipulation.

I have personally been part of the life of an addict and I will use some of what I experienced as an example. A very good friend of mine, due to things beyond his direct control, became an addict in his adulthood. What is meant by that is he began to live his life as if he were still a teenager. Its here were my example of how addicts will manipulate falls into place.

As we have seen, guilt is one method where an emotional manipulator will use in order to successfully get what that manipulator is trying for. With my friend, he was trying to get money in order to feed his addiction. I'm not talking about a few dollars here and there. He was spending somewhere in the area of $100 to $250 per day on drugs. Although he did have an income, it wasn't sufficient enough for these expenditures. So, he went to his mother for money. At first, she was able to tell him no. Then he began the guilt tactics in his manipulation. He used mistakes that his parents had made against them. He was able to identify those things from his past which bothered his mother the most. It didn't take long before he had turned his mom into a total enabler and this began her emotional downfall.

Addicts think differently than everyone else. He just wanted the drugs he felt that he needed. Although it wasn't his intention to hurt her, that's exactly what he did. He would remind her of some time back when he was a kid where things were not especially rosy. His father hadn't been the best dad and that is what he brought up. He didn't hesitate to bring those things up with her. She would jump at his every word. He played the emotional manipulation card well and, because of this, created an enabler that helped him drag out his addiction for years.

One of the best things that an emotional manipulator can use to lead another is love. This is just as, if not more, powerful than fear. This form of manipulation is probably the most damaging. It towers over blackmail and other trifling techniques. Love is a powerful motivator and this can be tweaked to be very unhealthy. Eventually, he regained his life, dropped the drugs, and is now spending what life he and his mother have in order to make amends to her and his entire family.

Other relationships are also subject to emotional manipulation. Unhealthy marriages are one example. In these relationships, usually one of the two will be the manipulator and the other his or her target. This is a very one-sided relationship that commonly is one person living only to please the other. The other will continuously take and take until there is nothing left. He or she will use whatever tactics are necessary to keep this going. Of course, there is almost always severe and irrefutable damage done to one of the two. This not only leads to divorce but can lead to much worse. It can lead to one of them being destroyed for the remainder of their life.

Now, let's look at one area where both psychological and emotional manipulation can occur simultaneously. We have all heard of cults but what do we actually know about them and those in which are affected. Cults, and those harmed by them, are widely misunderstood. There are many myths associated with cults and unfair stereotyping of those who are former members of them. Nevertheless, cults, and cult leaders, are prime examples of manipulators who use all of the available tactics in order to control their subjects.

What are some of the myths that are associated with cults? Here are a few. People can just leave if they are in a cult and wish not to be. Only stupid or non-assertive people join cults. Cults are based on religion. Cults are strange and their members are anti-social and usually outcasts. These are just a few. Now, let's look at the truth and how manipulation plays a key role in the cult leader's abilities in controlling members.

I remember learning about the cult leader Jim Jones and how he led over 900 followers, a third of them children, to commit mass suicide. In truth, not all of them drank the poison. Some were shot. They were the people who refused to drink poison because they wanted to live. How did they wind up in that situation, to begin with? It's complicated and is another topic that an entire series of books could be written. Here is a short summary.

Jones was very charismatic and intelligent. He was able to identify, or be mindful, of the wants and needs of people specific to that time and location. He was able to identify with those people who would follow him and he made them truly believe that he would be the one to lead them to better lives. He did this through manipulation and persuasion. He was both honest in some things and dishonest in others. In the beginning, the cult wasn't the way it had become at the end. As with all successful manipulators, he had to slowly progress in his power and he had to demonstrate extreme patience. After making them believe he was best for their lives and it was in their best interest to follow him, he began to place more control over them. The members were virtually prisoners by the end. They had invested all of their financial, emotional, and psychological resources into the cult and now we're trapped. Then Jones became dark and his mental health drastically declined. We say to each other that there is no way we could harm a child, especially our own child, or anyone else for that matter. However, by the time the mass suicide took place, they had no choice. It was poison or a bullet. A horrible truth but a real example of the power that a manipulator can gain and the destruction that can come as a result.

Now that we have taken a look down that dark path, let's come back to the lighter side of persuasion. Here is something to think about. Reviewing some previous information in this book, what is the first step in persuasion and manipulation? First, you need to find out what it is that you are wanting. Then you need to find a way to make your target feel as if he or she needs or wants the same. If not the same, a way for your target to think that he or she will somehow benefit from what you are trying to get them to do. You need to make it enticing. This does not have to be a lie. This is especially relevant to the workplace. There is probably nothing that will benefit you, while at work, that will not also benefit someone else. Use this to your advantage.

If you are truly intelligent and able to read and understand others, you will probably be able to identify reasons for that person to go along with your wishes and those reasons are genuine. You won't need to go to the dark place of manipulation. You will be able to simply persuade someone else based on joint benefits. A good word to remember is conglomeration. This means to bring together. If you have the ability to cause someone else to make a decision and you have done this without lying, harming another, and with integrity, you have proven yourself to be a true master of persuasion without gaining the stigma of being a trifling manipulator.

Chapter 11: Some Other Conspiracy Theories (Some Absurd, Some Credible)

6 Conspiracy Theories Surrounding the Denver Airport

On February 28, 1995, the Denver International Airport opened its doors and its airstrips to the general public after falling over a year behind schedule and investing a reported $2 billion more than its original budget had dictated.

The huge new airport didn't just use up a ton of money and time-- it also took up a ton of space: two decades later, it is still the biggest airport in the United States by location (53 square miles) with the longest public use runway readily available in the nation (runway 16R/34L is 16,000 feet long-- around three miles). DIA changed Denver's old Stapleton International Airport, and that was plagued by problems (runways too close together, a general lack of space for necessary growth), and its creation helped meet some basic needs that Stapleton just couldn't. Denver needed more room to serve the numerous airline companies that had made-- and wanted to make-- the Mile High City a center of operations, and DIA did just that.

That all noises normal enough, right? A city needed a brand-new airport, and it got one, even though it took a lot more cash and time than originally prepared, as so typically happens with massive public works (although there's some argument as to who actually financed the airport, but we'll get to that). But for the last 20 years, people have just wondered if DIA-- giant, pricey, odd DIA-- is home to something far more sinister ... like a conspiracy. Or a lot of conspiracies.

1. The Runway Shapes

Although one of the underlying themes of the various conspiracy theories relating to DIA holds that Stapleton was a great airport and didn't really need to be replaced, there's one inarguable point: the runways at Stapleton were not smartly set out. The parallel runways were actually too close together for safe landing in bad weather, which occurred around 150 days a year and cut the number of arrivals an hour from 80 to 36. DIA does not have the same issue, but it does have something far more dubious: a shape that many individuals have observed looks strangely enough like a swastika, at least from the air. Handled its own, such a shape could be brushed off as being just an actually awful piece of planning, but combined with everything else, all of it looks very peculiar certainly.

2. The Markings

The airport bears a series of "unusual" markings on its floors that some people really believe symbolize a brand-new strain of liver disease that could be used in natural warfare. In reality, the majority of the signs are drawn from Navajo language or are pulled from the table of elements of aspects.

3. The Commitment Marker

There is one very odd marker that is hard to overlook: a commitment marker and capstone that is been positioned over a time capsule (which apparently consists of a credit card, Colorado flag, and DIA opening day papers, amongst lots of other things) that's set to be opened in 2094. The symbols on the marker are related to the Freemasons, a charitable company that's typically subject to their own conspiracy theories. The marker also discusses the "New World Airport Commission," an organization that does not actually exist (or does it? our brains are spinning!) but seems taking credit for building the entire airport. Still, the contributors noted as part of the so-called NWAC, and that includes an architecture firm and a metal company, do exist. And they just make structures and metals. Well, probably.

4. and 5. The Tunnels and the Underground Bunker

The airport is home to a number of tunnels, including a cable car that goes between concourses and an unsuccessful automated baggage system. That all sounds typical enough, but there is definitely something strange about that automated luggage system-- primarily, that it cost a lot of cash and after that never actually worked. The system, and that failed pretty spectacularly when it was first tested and just never got better, was just one of the reasons for DIA's postponed opening. By 2005, the majority of the airport's concourses had abandoned it absolutely, making both its puffed up cost and long delays just feel like a lot more of a failure-- or at least an actually odd way to cover up the structure of tunnels.

But where do the tunnels go? Maybe to some kind of underground bunker? The majority of the people who believe in the various conspiracy theories regarding DIA appear to actually think that the airport is actually the head office for something far nastier than just an airport-- like the New World Order or our own American government. This idea might sound pretty wild-- just because the place is huge? just because of all that unusual stuff in the airport?-- but there is something very weird to back it up: buried structures.

As the story goes, when DIA was first being built, five massive buildings were built somehow incorrectly. Rather than being exploded or otherwise dismantled, they were buried. Although theorists say that a construction worker eventually blew the whistle on this very odd practice, finding his original testament on the topic is practically unrealistic.

6. The Horse Statue and the Weird Murals

Conspiracy theories aside, it is tough to deny the weirdness of DIA's unofficial mascot-- an enormous horse statue called "Blue Mustang" that has already killed at least one man. At 32 feet tall and 9000 pounds (it's constructed of fiberglass), "Blue Mustang" is huge and enforcing, and its glowing red eyes don't help matters. This thing is huge and actually creepy-- and it killed the man who made it. Truly. Artist Luis Jimenez died in 2006 when a piece of the sculpture's head broke off and severed an artery in his leg.

Leo Tanguma's 2 murals, and that use up large swathes of wallspace in DIA's baggage claim, might have some good names-- they are called "Children of the World Imagine Peace" and "In Peace and Harmony with Nature," respectively-- but their actual content is frightening. Death-masked soldiers stalk children with weapons, animals are dead and kept under glass, and the whole world seeks to have been damaged. As if being at the airport is not bad enough.

To his credit, the story of Tanguma's murals ends on a very happy note-- with all that peace and harmony stuff-- and the artist himself has said, "I have children sleeping amid the remains of war and this warmonger is eliminating the dove of peace, but the kids are imagining something better in the future and their little dream goes behind the general and continues behind this group of people, and the kids are dreaming that [peace] will happen sooner or later. See how the little dream becomes something actually gorgeous, that one day the nations of the world will abandon war and come together." Still, the last spot anyone wants to see representations of death and destruction in an airport.

The JFK Assassination

This much we can stipulate: President John F. Kennedy was assassinated on Nov. 22, 1963, struck by 2 bullets-- one in the head, one in the neck-- while riding in an open-topped limo through Dealey Plaza in Dallas. Lee Harvey Oswald was charged with eliminating him, and a presidential commission headed by Chief Justice Earl Warren found that Oswald acted alone.

That conclusion hasn't satisfied requirements with the general public. A 2003 ABC News poll found that 70% of Americans actually believe Kennedy's death was the outcome of a broader plot. The trajectory of the bullets, some say, didn't square with Oswald's perch on the 6th floor of the Texas School Book Depository. Others suggest a 2nd shooter-- perhaps on the grassy knoll of Dealey Plaza-- took part in the shooting. Others really believe in an even wider conspiracy. Was Kennedy killed by CIA representatives acting either out of anger over the Bay of Pigs or at the wish of Vice President Lyndon Johnson? By KGB operatives? Mobsters mad at Kennedy's brother for initiating the prosecution of organized crime rings? Speculation over one of history's most well-known political assassinations is such a well-known parlor game that many people have taken the rumors to heart: just 32% of those surveyed by ABC actually believe Oswald carried out the killing on his own.

9/11 Cover-Up

Not since the JFK assassination has there been a national tragedy so heavily imprinted in American minds-- or that has given rise to quite as tons of alternative explanations. While videos and photos of the two planes striking the World Trade Center towers are famous around the world, the large profusion of documentary proof has only provided much more fodder for conspiracy theories.

A May 2006 Zogby survey found that 42% of Americans actually believed that the federal government and the 9/11 commission "concealed or refused to examine critical evidence that contradicts their official explanation of the September 11th attacks." Why had the army failed to obstruct the pirated planes? Had the federal government provided a "stand down" order, to decrease disturbance with a secret plan to destroy the structures and blame it on Islamic terrorists? In 2005, Popular Mechanics published a huge investigation of comparable claims and reactions to them. The reporting team found that the North American Aerospace Defense Command (NORAD) didn't have a history of having fighter jets prepped and prepared to intercept airplane that had gone off path. And while the group found no proof that the federal government had planned the attacks, absence of evidence has seldom stopped conspiracy theorists right before.

Area 51 and the Aliens

We may have Tang thanks to the space program, but who gave us such developments as the Stealth fighter and Kevlar? Aliens, obviously. Conspiracy theorists really believe that the remains of crashed UFO spacecrafts are saved at Area 51, a Flying force base about 150 miles from Las Vegas, where government researchers reverse-engineer the aliens' highly advanced technology. Fodder for this has come from a variety of supposed UFO sightings in the area and testimony from a retired Army colonel who says he was admitted to extraterrestrial materials gathered from an alien spacecraft that crashed in Roswell, N.M. Some believe that the government studies time travel at Area 51, also referred to as Groom Lake or Dreamland.

The government has developed sophisticated aircraft and weapons systems at nearby Nellis Air Force Base, and that includes Stealth bombers and reconnaissance planes. And the government's main line-- that the details of Area 51 are classified for purposes of national security-- is only seen as more evidence that the military is hiding aliens or alien spacecraft.

Secret Societies Control the World

If you were truly a member of the global élite, you 'd know this already: the world is governed by a powerful, deceptive few. Lots of the rest of us peons have heard that in 2004 both prospects for the White Home were members of Yale University's deceptive Skull and Bones society, lots of whose members have increased to effective positions. But Skull and Bones is little potatoes compared with the mysterious cabals that inhabit virtually every catbird seat, from the passages of government to the conference rooms of Wall Street.

Take the Illuminati, a sect said to have originated in 18th century Germany and which is supposedly accountable for the pyramid-and-eye sign adorning the $1 costs: they mean to foment world wars to enhance the argument for the creation of a worldwide federal government (which would, naturally, be Satanic in nature). Or consider the Freemasons, who tout their group as the "oldest and biggest around the world fraternity" and boast alumni like George Washington. Some think that despite contributing stacks of cash to charity, they're secretly outlining your undoing at Masonic temples across the world. Or maybe, some theorize, the guys pulling the strings aren't concealed in shadow at all. They might be the intelligentsia on the Council on Foreign Relations, a cadre of policy wonks who allegedly count their objectives as releasing an erudite bimonthly journal and developing a unified world government--not necessarily in that order.

The Moon Landings Were Fabricated

It's now been nearly four decades since Neil Armstrong took his "huge leap for humanity"-- if, that is, he ever set foot off this world. Skeptics say the U.S. federal government, desperate to beat the Russians in the space race, faked the lunar landings, with Armstrong and Buzz Aldrin acting out their mission on a secret film set, located (depending on the concept) either high in the Hollywood Hills or deep within Area 51. With the photos and videos of the Apollo missions only readily available through NASA, there's no independent confirmation that the lunar landings were anything but a hoax.

The smoking weapon? Film of Aldrin planting a waving American flag on the moon, and that critics say proves that he was not in space. The flag's movement, they say, clearly shows the presence of wind, and that is impossible in a vacuum. NASA says Aldrin was twisting the flagpole to get the moon dirt, which triggered the flag to move. (And never ever mind that astronauts have revived hundreds of individually confirmed moon rocks.) Theorists have even suggested that filmmaker Stanley Kubrick may have helped NASA fake the first lunar landing, considered that his 1968 movie 2001: An Area Odessey proves that the technology existed back then to artificially develop a spacelike set. And when it comes to Virgil I. Grissom, Edward H. White and Roger B. Chaffee-- 3 astronauts who passed away in a fire while testing equipment for the first moon mission? They were carried out by the USA federal government, and that feared they were about to reveal the truth.

Improbable as the hoax theory might seem, a 1999 Gallup poll showed that it's relatively resilient: 6% of Americans said they thought the lunar landings were fake, and 5% said they were uncertain.

Jesus and Mary Magdalene

Jesus and Mary Magdalene might have been married, or so says the Gospel of Philip. Sure, it is the basic plot of The Da Vinci Code (the thriller also wraps in conspiracy shibboleths like Opus Dei and the Knights Templar for great measure)-- but the theory finds its basis in writings from the Gnostic Gospels, which were discovered in 1945 and whose authenticity religious specialists still contest. In the Gospel of Philip, Mary Magdalene, who is described as Jesus' koinonos, a Greek term for "companion" or "partner," is portrayed as being closer to Jesus than any other apostle.

Conclusion

Thank you for reading this book! Let's hope that you have finished the book with a deeper knowledge of Dark Psychology as well as the numerous study sub-sections that have been developed over the years. The details in this insightful and enlightening guide have been gathered from the most knowledgeable and respected sources so that our readers can be assertive in their newly gained knowledge. We genuinely hope that you will not only feel better educated about the dark aspect of human psychology and that you will be armed with the resources you need to improve your full capability in persuasion or other techniques, but also that you have completed our guide with the urge to know more and never stop yearning for knowledge. Now you have a better understanding of what to do and how to achieve it, the next move is simply to bring your newly found skill into effect!

www.ingramcontent.com/pod-product-compliance
Lightning Source LLC
Chambersburg PA
CBHW071431070526
44578CB00001B/74